THE
SECRET
LANGUAGE
OF DOGS

VICTORIA STILWELL

star of *It's Me or The Dog*

THE
SECRET
LANGUAGE
OF DOGS

Unlocking the Canine Mind
for a Happier Pet

hamlyn

CONTENTS

I dedicate this book to my father-in-law, Van Iden Zeiler Jr

Your kindness and devotion will never be forgotten.

INTRODUCTION

For centuries, scientists believed that only humans had emotions and conscious mental processes, whereas animals were purely automated beings with no psychological processes of any significance. This belief was firmly entrenched until modern science challenged it.[1] Fascinating new research suggests that animals' mental abilities are similar to people's – depending, of course, on what a particular species needs in order to adapt and survive.

We live in an exciting time of scientific research and discovery. The last ten years have seen an explosion in the study of canine behaviour and cognition, thanks to universities and research centres around the world. The minds of dogs are being explored like never before, and the findings are proving once and for all just how intelligent, emotional and complex dogs are.

Dogs have coexisted with humans for thousands of years, and as they have adapted, so has their ability to communicate with us. By paying close attention to our vocal and physical language, dogs have evolved a rich social intelligence and a physical and vocal language as complex and subtle as our own. Like humans, dogs communicate consciously and unconsciously, using body and vocal signals that reflect what they are thinking and feeling. These signals communicate intent and ensure dogs' personal safety by affecting behaviour in others.

Understanding what your dog is saying is the key to building a strong relationship. But not all language is easy to read, and some subtle signals are hard to interpret. Gestures or actions that we assume mean one thing can actually be the dog telling us something completely different. Understanding and communicating effectively with your dog is vital for helping him to learn and for strengthening the bond between you. And along the way, you'll find that canine language is as beautiful as it is complex.

This book will help you to not only understand how your dog thinks and feels but also appreciate his needs so that he can live confidently in your world.

UNDERSTANDING AND TEACHING YOUR DOG

Building a secure bond, communicating effectively and understanding how your dog perceives the world will help you teach your dog successfully. And while this book attempts to interpret the many intricacies of canine language, there will always be behaviour that is harder to define or explain. We are now realizing, thanks to years of observation and scientific study, not only how incredible dogs are, but also how important it is to treat them with kindness and respect. For decades, dog training has focused on punitively forcing dogs

to 'obey', which has prevented them from truly learning, thinking and making their own choices. Harsh training methods have produced a population of emotionally stressed dogs that display worrying and sometimes dangerous behaviour. Fortunately, the positive teaching movement is fast gaining momentum, and as more people choose humane, fear-free techniques to teach their dogs, this in turn encourages learning, builds trust and enhances confidence. Dog lovers all over the world are discovering that teaching humanely is not only fun but also enhances their dogs' natural learning abilities and strengthens the bond between them.

THE PROBLEM WITH PUNISHMENT

Punitive training is based on an outdated theory that incorrectly assumes dogs need to be shown who is 'alpha', 'the boss' or 'pack leader'. People are led to believe that dogs display dominant behaviour because they want to be at the top of the family hierarchy. While groups of dogs do form a social hierarchy, the myth that dogs are intent on achieving a dominant status over humans has pervaded the dog training world for years, with unfortunate consequences. If people think their dogs are trying to dominate them, then people are more likely to dominate them in return until, according to the theory, their dogs learn their place in the pack. The resulting confrontation damages the human/animal bond, inhibits a dog's ability to learn and encourages aggressive behaviour. In any event, the intricate planning needed to prepare a strategy to achieve this mutiny is something that even dogs, with their high level of intelligence, just can't handle. How do we know this? The secret lies in the cerebral cortex – the layer of grey matter in the brain that covers the cerebral hemispheres and is responsible for brain function, including sensation, voluntary muscle movement, thought, reasoning and memory. A dog's cerebral cortex is not as intricate as a human's, so dogs can't create strategies with such complexity.

Techniques that traditional trainers use include devices that hurt the dog to curb unwanted behaviour – such as choke, prong or shock collars – and training methods that intimidate and frighten the dog, including physical punishment and restraint techniques. However, science is clear on the ineffectiveness of these techniques. Studies have shown that when a dog is punished by being pinned down on his back or side in an 'alpha roll', his body releases cortisol. Cortisol is a stress hormone produced by the amygdala – the brain's integrative centre for emotions, emotional behaviour and motivation – that readies the body for danger. The high cortisol level overwhelms the dog's brain, interfering with rational thought. A person might think that when they hold their dog down and the dog 'gives up' that he is submitting or becoming calm; in fact, the dog is becoming more stressed and shuts down. When a dog shuts down, he can't learn, so while punishment might suppress behaviour for that moment, the dog learns nothing. He also becomes more stressed, and his behaviour never truly changes because he is given no alternative choice.[2]

Unfortunately, many dog trainers have bought into the dominance myth. While these trainers vehemently defend their beliefs to justify the use of force, positive trainers like me regularly pick up the pieces that compulsion trainers (as they are known) leave in their wake, and it can take months or

even years to rehabilitate dogs back to a healthy state. The evidence is clear: fear will break your dog. Fortunately, modern science has given us a nuanced understanding of how dogs truly think, feel and socialize – and it has shown us a new way forwards.

DOMINANCE

Does this mean that a social hierarchy is unimportant to a dog? Well, not quite. Dominance is important in canine social relationships, but they commonly use dominant language to de-escalate a social situation. For dogs, a healthy social order avoids conflict and is flexible, depending on what matters to each dog. Rather than increasing aggression, dominant behaviour evolved as a way to actively avoid it because behaving aggressively can get a dog hurt and even threaten its very survival. Unlike humans in their dominant behaviour over dogs, which can be physically violent, a truly dominant dog might exert his dominance by using non-violent behaviour to defuse a situation. A simple look, a paw touch or a head draped over the shoulders of another dog may ensure that the dog using the gesture maintains priority access to resources.

Social order works well in a multi-dog household if different things matter to different dogs. Ritualized greeting displays enforce which dog gets priority access over what resource: food, water, attention, a comfy resting spot. However, some dogs ignore social order and challenge the status quo. These dogs often have little experience of healthy social relationships, and they tend to use language that is psychologically intimidating and physically violent, causing disagreements and fights.

So when a person physically punishes their dog to show their status as 'pack leader',

DOMINANCE/CONTROL: a head draped over the shoulders of another dog

they're not replicating the behaviour of a truly dominant dog that controls without the use of physical force. They are actually playing the role of a socially incompetent bully.

This means that if you teach your dog correctly while building a good relationship, there is no reason to use punitive techniques. Dogs are trying to survive and thrive in our domestic world. Veterinarians and veterinary behaviourists are warning against the use of punishment-based methods that compromise not only a dog's ability to learn but his chance of living successfully in a human world.[3]

POSITIVE TRAINING

When we follow the positive training philosophy, we encourage dogs and other animals to learn using humane, fear-free techniques that help them problem solve. We never use force and intimidation because positive training puts the emphasis on teaching dogs what to do rather than punishing them for not doing what we want. This is a much more effective way to promote learning. Thankfully, it also helps rehabilitate dogs with anxieties, fears, aggressive behaviour and phobias.

By giving dogs some control over their own choices while gently guiding them, we allow them to adapt to novel situations and environments much more successfully. Allowing dogs to learn what works in certain situations builds their confidence while providing a healthy balance of self-discovery. This gentle guidance allows dogs to become more socially adept and emotionally balanced. We may not be naturally inclined to give up control so easily, but maintaining a good balance of independent and dependent learning makes a significant positive difference in the lives of all dogs.

There are many effective teaching techniques. Some dogs learn well through problem-solving exercises; others learn better through clicker training, lure-reward or techniques that 'catch' behaviour. Some trainers prefer a more cognitive approach, establishing a bond first rather than having dogs work for human approval. Others take a more behavioural approach, teaching life skills through cues and techniques like 'shaping', whereby actions and behaviours are built through reward-based training. I like to do both: focus on building a bond as well as teaching cues without pressure, guiding dogs to learn and have fun while doing so. No matter how we choose to humanely and effectively change our dog's behaviour and teach necessary life skills, we should always respect the dog's autonomy.

Unfortunately, dog training professionals on both sides of the debate are now so focused on 'training' dogs that some dogs have lost the ability to think for themselves, relying completely on people to direct them. These naturally independent problem solvers are being overwhelmed and overtrained. The positive community is well ahead of the compulsion community when it comes to encouraging dogs to think and problem solve, but we can still benefit from taking the pressure off and doing less. Shifting away from more structured training and towards developing dogs' natural social skills and problem-solving abilities will create even happier and more confident pets.

CREATING BOUNDARIES

Contrary to popular opinion, *positive* does not mean 'permissive'. Positive trainers and people who subscribe to the philosophy do believe in setting boundaries for dogs and telling them 'no' when necessary, just as they would with a child. They use rewards in the form of food, praise, play and toys to encourage and recognize good behaviour, as well as humane techniques to discourage negative behaviour. To create boundaries, I may (1) use vocal cues to interrupt and redirect negative to positive behaviour, (2) remove the dog from a volatile situation, (3) withhold a reward, or (4) simply ignore behaviour I don't like. Most importantly, I set dogs up for success by giving them choices and teaching alternative behaviours they can use instead. I put the emphasis on learning new skills rather than punishment.

The beauty of positive training is that it works with any dog, regardless of breed or drive, and promotes the development of a strong human/canine bond. Even if your dog is a slow learner, she will be happier and have the confidence needed to cope with your human domestic world if she is taught humanely, with patience and understanding. And the best way to understand your dog is by learning how she thinks and experiences the world and what her body language means – which is what this book is about. Read on!

PART I

THE SECRET INNER EXPERIENCE OF DOGS

The unique relationship between human and dog has overcome the species divide for generations. And thanks to the great advances being made in the field of animal behavioural and cognitive science, we now have a clearer insight into the secret inner lives of our canine companions. There is significant evidence to support what those of us who love and work with dogs already know: our dogs are thinking, feeling and emotional beings with exceptional learning abilities and species-specific intelligence. Their incredible adaptability and desire to be by our side at all times is what makes the relationship we have with them so extraordinary. This section reveals the unique way dogs experience the world around them, and it is a crucial foundation for this book's later section on decoding the meaning of their vocal and body language.

CHAPTER 1

THE LOVING DOG

Thousands of years of domestication have played a significant role in the human/ dog relationship, and as dogs have evolved with humans, they have adapted and acquired the abilities they need to live with us successfully. Among their many cognitive capabilities, dogs can make inferences, understand human gestures, read our intentions, and be sensitive to our attentional and emotional states. They can also understand easy words and imitate human physical language, and they may also be able to empathize with our emotions. I will focus more on these throughout the book, but for now it's important to understand how dogs have evolved to become not only the most successful domesticated animal species on the planet but also our closest and dearest companions.

Successful evolution relies on natural selection; that is, how adaptable a species is to the changing environment around them. In terms of evolutionary adaptation, dogs are extraordinary. These amazing animals have successfully evolved for thousands of years as their wolf-like capabilities were transformed by the challenges of living with humans.[1]

Cohabitation created a mutually beneficial relationship for dogs and humans. Dogs were an effective alarm system – guarding settlements, crops and livestock – and they helped their human companions hunt and gather food. Dogs were also the first effective rubbish disposal system – eating the scraps that humans left behind. However, their most important job was and still is that of companion and friend. Dogs just make us feel good, and life is better when we share it with them.

DOES YOUR DOG LOVE YOU?

When a dog gazes at you with his big brown eyes, greets you excitedly at the end of the day and snuggles next to you when you sleep, is this proof that he loves you, or is he just forming an attachment for the safety, comfort and food you provide? Humans love to anthropomorphize – that is, attribute human characteristics, motivations or behaviours onto other species – and while this usually poses no problem, it becomes an issue when the human desire to dominate others or ascend in rank is used to explain canine behaviour, or when a dog is treated too much like a human baby or child. What is certain is that when a dog shows 'loving' behaviour, the mechanisms at play are similar to those at play when a person feels love.

Oxytocin is the hormone responsible for social bonding. When a mother gives birth and holds her newborn baby in her arms for the first time, the release of oxytocin, among other hormones, is responsible for bonding her to her baby. When two people fall in love, they experience a number of physical symptoms – such as loss of appetite and increased heart rate and sweat production – all thanks to oxytocin. We shouldn't be surprised, then, by a 2003 study showing that oxytocin also plays a large part in the social and emotional bonding between dogs and humans.[2] When dogs were petted by their owners, oxytocin levels in their

blood rose within five to twenty-four minutes of the petting session, proving that positive social contact is beneficial for both species.

Oxytocin also strengthens social memories in the brain, allowing dogs to bond during social interactions as well as to remember the experience. However, this might not always be a positive thing, as research shows that oxytocin can also cause emotional pain.[3] This hormone appears to be the reason we recall stressful situations long after the event, and these memories can trigger fear and anxiety in the future. If a social experience is negative or stressful, the hormone activates a part of the brain that intensifies the memory. Oxytocin also makes us more susceptible to feeling fearful and anxious during stressful upcoming events.[4] So be aware of how oxytocin and other powerful hormones can influence positive and negative experiences in your dog's life. Help your dog become socially and environmentally confident by giving her plenty of positive experiences in different situations.

BE A SECURE ATTACHMENT

A dog's attachment to a human is like a child's to a parent. In fact, dogs behave very similarly to young children in that they are more apt to explore new situations and environments when a human they trust is nearby than if that human is absent. This attachment in children is demonstrated by the 'strange situation' test, in which a child will confidently explore a strange environment when the mother is present but will stop exploring and anxiously wait for the mother to return if she leaves for a period of time. When dogs were put through a similar test, they behaved in exactly the same way.[5] I don't mean to say every dog will have a similar reaction, but dogs with high human attachment will actually have more confidence to explore novel situations if someone they know and trust is close by.

THE LANGUAGE OF LOVE

LOVE: relaxed, fluid body language and blinking eyes

The language of a loving dog is easy to understand because it's very similar to how humans express affection. Apart from the human hug, which can sometimes feel threatening to a dog (especially from a stranger), loving behaviour is shown through the dog's desire to be physically close to a person. Relaxed, fluid body language, gentle, blinking eyes and a calm, happy demeanour are all indications that a dog feels safe and comfortable in a person's presence.

CHAPTER 2

THE THINKING DOG

Cognition can be defined as the way you and your dog perceive the world around you, and cognition celebrates many types of intelligence. Learning is influenced by the environment in which a dog is raised. Dogs reared in less nurturing environments tend to be less reliant on a person's attempts to communicate physically or vocally, whereas dogs raised in close contact with humans tend to rely much more on people to guide and direct them. The more you understand your dog's cognitive style, the easier it will be to teach him. If your dog finds learning difficult or is slow to pick up on your cues, he's not being stupid – he simply learns in a way different to what you might expect.

Every dog can learn, but dogs – like humans – learn in different ways and at different speeds. Some dogs will pick up human cues very quickly, while others may pay more attention to the environment around them. The latter are not being disrespectful or stubborn but are easily distracted or feel the need to keep vigilant to ensure survival. This might be because they are genetically predisposed to be more sensitive to the surrounding environment or because they are so tempted by the smells around them that they are too distracted to focus.

Reasoning is a dog's ability to solve a problem when he can't see an answer and has to imagine a solution.[1] Dogs are natural-born problem solvers, a skill that is vital for tracking and finding prey and negotiating environment.

Dogs that are more independent thinkers tend to be better at solving problems because they rely less on others to help them. Modern dog training has certainly helped dogs adapt to living with humans, but it has also created dogs that think less independently and rely more on human beings to direct them or help them solve a problem. Lack of socialization, punitive handling and anxiety or fear issues also compromise a dog's ability to think clearly.

Numerous studies have been done to assess canine reasoning skills, which usually involves setting up problems for dogs to solve. For example, food is put behind a glass revolving door with long barriers on either side. After the challenge is set, a dog is brought into the room and encouraged to find the food, then left to do so independently. Reasoning skills are assessed based on whether the dog solves the problem by pushing the door with his nose to get to the food or by going around the barriers. Neither method is judged right or wrong and the dog is timed to see how quickly he can solve the problem. Most dogs are very good at working the problem and finding a solution without being shown.[2]

MEMORY

Memory is crucial for problem solving, hunting of prey, smell recognition, facial recognition and general learning. Dogs need to memorize environmental landmarks so they can find their way around as well as construct mental maps of where these landmarks are located. Although dogs use visual markers to navigate their surroundings, they rely more heavily on how things smell. This mental mapping is important for remembering territory and territorial boundaries as well as for being able to reach a food source or an area of comfort and safety.

Dogs also need to have a good working memory if they have to find food for themselves. They have to remember that if the prey they are chasing goes behind a rock and disappears, it might still be there even though they can't see it.

It's believed not only that dogs have good olfactory memory and can remember smells for years afterwards, but also that smell is linked to their emotional memory, just as it is in humans. The smell of a veterinary surgery may always elicit negative emotions, whereas the odour of a favoured person triggers happiness and joy. Auditory memory is also important and is especially useful when it comes to remembering the sound, tone and pitch of a human vocal signal that is linked to a certain action or behaviour.

TOP TIP

You can test your dog's working memory by showing your dog where you are hiding a treat or toy, taking him out of the room or area for a minute, and then bringing him back and asking him to get the treat or toy. Most dogs will remember where the lure is hidden rather than using their sense of smell to find it. Try testing his longer-term memory by gradually increasing the time he is out of range.

Dogs can not only recognize the voices of people they know but also learn and remember that different vocal pitches and tones mean different things. Their physical reading skills can help them determine what human vocalizations mean, and because people tend to speak in higher pitches when they are being affectionate and lower pitches when they are upset or angry, it is easy for dogs to learn the difference and respond accordingly. You can help your dog learn by being consistent with your vocal pitch as well as being aware of how to use tone when talking to your dog or giving cues. In general, the type of cue will determine the type of tone and pitch you use. You can use high-energy vocalizations to excite your dog into playing, for example, or to get your dog to come back to you when you call; use medium tones for everyday cues such as 'wait' by the food bowl or 'stay' by the front door when a guest is entering. You can use lower tones to tell your dog how you feel about a certain behaviour, but take care not to frighten him into compliance. The canine memory is so good that he will truly remember and recognize the difference!

Dogs that have been raised in positive, stimulating environments tend to have better memory function than dogs that have been raised in social isolation because the more pleasant experiences a dog has in early life, the more chances its brain has to develop.[3]

HOW TO SPEAK DOG

HIGH TONES = excited, affectionate and playful

MEDIUM TONES = everyday cues like 'stay'

LOW TONES = serious (use sparingly)

HOW DOGS LEARN

The way dogs learn depends on a number of factors, including how they were bred, how instinctively skilled they are, the influence of hormones and chemicals, early experience, and how they are raised. Dogs are a highly adaptable species because they have good problem-solving skills. These have developed because they are needed for survival and are particularly useful for seeking out, hunting and catching prey. Some dogs are more adaptively intelligent than others, but they can learn problem-solving skills by watching other dogs or humans. While some dogs are independent thinkers and are less reliant on human intervention to help them problem solve, others rely solely on humans to guide them.

Dogs are learning all the time, not just when they're being taught – in fact, all life is learning, particularly for young dogs, whose brains are like sponges soaking up the environment around them. And playtime offers one of the best learning experiences for any dog. Healthy play teaches dogs good social skills as well as the ability to restrain themselves. Using self-control in any situation, particularly during play, ensures that dogs can rehearse behaviours and roughhouse with the confidence that play will not escalate into something more serious. Dogs also learn good self-control skills when playing with humans. Tug is a great game as long as both dogs and humans follow the rules, winning and losing during the game, and the dog willingly drops the toy when the human asks him to.

TUG: healthy play

Dogs are great observers and learn socially from humans and other dogs. Occasionally they also learn social skills from a different animal species, highlighting their amazing ability to adapt. A problem is much easier to solve when a dog can see someone else solving it first, so if your dog is having a hard time working out how to do something, showing her how it's done can help her solve the problem.

TRAINING TIPS

You can teach your dog to trade and give up objects easily by making the whole experience a game. The 'Take it and drop it' cue teaches your dog to take something you give him and then drop it on cue; this can be hard for some dogs, especially with a high-value object such as a favourite toy or tug rope.

- Start with an object of low value and present it to your dog.

- When he opens his mouth to take the object, say 'Take it'.

- Allow him to play with the object, then present him with a duplicate that you have behind your back.

- As your dog drops the object he has in his mouth, say 'Drop it' and reward him with the duplicate that you have in your other hand, saying 'Take it'.

Keep repeating this exercise; when your dog is consistently complying, you can gradually build up with toys of higher value.

- If your dog does not want to give up the higher-value toy, walk away from him, produce a new toy and start directing all your interest to that new toy while you play with it.

- When your dog's curiosity gets the better of him, he will come over and give up the toy he has in his mouth.

- Immediately reward his decision by giving him the new toy and repeating the 'Take it', 'Drop it' sequence.

LEARNING: following your body language cues

I love teaching dogs through imitation. This technique has become more popular with trainers like Claudia Fugazza who teach dogs based on their cognitive skills. Her 'Do As I Do' method focuses on teaching dogs various actions by having humans perform them first and then asking the dog to imitate the action. It's a wonderful method that allows dogs to think and problem solve rather than being lured, shaped or cued into performing an action or behaviour.[4]

Operant conditioning teaches a dog to link a specific action or behaviour such as sitting to a vocal cue or hand signal. This type of learning is very popular in the dog-training world and is highly effective when it comes to building a language of communication between the two species.

Classical conditioning or associative learning is automatic. For example, a dog learns that the rustle of his food bag means he'll get fed, or your approaching a certain drawer means you are fetching his lead to take him for a walk.

Habituation reduces a dog's anxiety in reaction to unexpected events. Habituating dogs to different environments or situations by continual positive exposure – such as being groomed while being fed delicious food – reduces the likelihood of a fear reaction in a similar situation. If a dog habituates or adapts well to new environments or the approach of new people, for example, he is more likely to cope with the unpredictability and confusing nature of human domestic life.

Sensitization refers to repeated exposure to a stimulus that causes an animal to become more reactive to it. This is commonly seen when dogs lunge at other dogs walking past. A traumatic experience with any dog or lack of social interaction can be generalized to a fear of being around or socially interacting with all dogs, and the more dog encounters he has, the more reactive and fearful he will become.

Desensitization occurs when dogs are desensitized to a stimulus that they were previously sensitized to. Now the dog that fears other dogs begins to see that other dogs pose no threat. This can be achieved in a number of ways. Counter-conditioning is a system whereby dogs are slowly exposed to a stimulus they fear, creating an emotion that counters the emotion they previously felt. For example, the dog fearful of other dogs is exposed to other dogs in a controlled way, both physically and emotionally, and good things now happen to him when other dogs walk past. This builds up an association that is counter to the previous conditioned response. Counter-conditioning techniques work well with dogs that show aggressive behaviour and those that suffer from anxieties, fears and phobias.

LEARNING THROUGH MOTIVATION

To learn in our human world, dogs need to trust us and be willing and motivated to learn. This depends on their capacity to learn, attention span, reaction to distraction, ability to listen and focus, trust, sociability and self-control, as well as their ability to understand human communication signals.

The anticipation of a reward is almost more powerful than the reward itself. When the dog anticipates a reward, the seeking system of its brain (the hypothalamus) is more active and sensitive to any stimuli that predict a reward. Pleasure is linked to the limbic system, which is linked to the olfactory bulb, and the seeking system is connected to the dopamine learning system.

Dopamine is the chemical that gives dogs a natural high. Appetitive behaviours are linked to the seeking system, and the process of wanting 'lights up the brain like a Christmas tree'.[5] However, if you tap too much into your dog's appetite system, there is a chance he might become disengaged. You want to keep your dog 'wanting', so go easy on rewards, as too many can interfere with the behaviour itself. Similarly, because play is so motivating to some dogs, if you play too much with them, not only is it hard for them to come down from the natural high that play gives, but too much play will distract from what you want to teach your dog. Keep play sessions short when you're using them as rewards. Motivation can be learnt, and learning is fuelled by motivation.

Different breeds have adapted to do different things and therefore may learn in different ways. Scent games for a pug may be harder than for a beagle; auditory memory skills may be easier for a border collie than they are for a nose-driven basset hound.

SOCIAL LEARNING THROUGH COMMUNICATIVE GESTURES

The human/canine relationship is further strengthened by dogs' ability to read human communicative gestures as well as their sensitivity to our emotions. For example, dogs have a genetic capacity to learn from an early age what a human point means – something that is a lot harder for other animal species to do. Dogs have evolved to read our social and communicative gestures, as these are important for their survival. When a person reads a human face, for example, their eyes wander to the left, ending on the right-hand side of the face. This left gaze bias happens only when humans encounter faces, not objects, because the right-hand side of a face is better at expressing emotional states than the left. Studies at the University of Lincoln have shown that dogs also have this left gaze bias only when they look at a human face, not an object or the face of another dog. This ability may have developed as a way for dogs to keep themselves safe by reading when humans are angry or displeased with them.[6]

SENSORY LEARNING

Dogs can be taught a myriad of skills using their natural sensory abilities.
I call this kind of learning sensory education. Scent work is a great use of a
dog's natural scenting abilities to teach him to find hidden food, toys or odours
that have been left in different locations, allowing them to use their powerful
seeking skills and providing them much-needed mental enrichment. Any dog
can be taught to find a particular odour, especially when the odour is paired
with a reward such as a treat or a toy. Simply hiding some food or a toy in an
easy location and asking your dog to find it is beneficial and provides hours of
entertainment inside or outside the home.

Teaching through the auditory learning system can also help dogs in
many situations. For example, dogs that are scared of noises like thunder and
fireworks can be taught to tolerate these noises by using a certain type of music
to desensitize them. Music can actually help discharge a dog's central nervous

system by using frequency modulation. My Canine Noise Phobia Series, which uses the great research done by sound researcher Joshua Leeds and concert pianist Lisa Spector, demonstrates how sound can calm nervous or anxious dogs in almost any situation, from the car to the shelter.[7]

CAN YOU MAKE YOUR DOG MORE INTELLIGENT?

In the 1940s, Canadian psychologist Donald Hebb compared the learning ability of dogs reared as pets to those raised in a barren kennel environment. He discovered that the pet dogs learned faster, were less fearful and were therefore less stressed in novel situations than the poor pups that had not been so lucky. In fact, continuing research has shown that the brains of animals living in enriching environments are usually larger because new connections develop between existing neurons as a result of good experiences. Performing any kind of problem-solving activity makes it possible to grow new neural cells in areas of the brain associated with memory and learning.[8]

So is it possible to change the physiology of your dog's brain with more environmental enrichment – and thereby make your dog more intelligent? This would depend on what your dog finds enriching, what motivates him and what environments he can experience without being overwhelmed. The more freedom you can give your dog to interact with the world around him, the quicker he will learn and the less fearful he is likely to be. It stands to reason that by keeping the brain busy with good thinking and problem-solving activities like hide-and-seek, interactive toys and puzzles, and plenty of stimulating walks, you can reduce your dog's chances of experiencing anxiety, stress or fear in any kind of situation, regardless of your dog's age.

Remember, intelligence is measured by the skills a dog needs to adapt and survive in his environment. Understanding how dogs learn, as well as taking advantage of their problem-solving capabilities and amazing senses, will make it easier for you and your dog to understand each other. A dog that has a deeper connection with you will be more likely to listen to you when you need his attention and will find it easier living in your domestic world.

CHAPTER 3

THE EMOTIONAL DOG

The brain of a dog is similar to a human's in many ways. The limbic system in both controls major emotions – such as fear and anger – and the basic neural chemistry is the same. For example, recent research has shown striking similarities in the ways that dog and human brains process emotionally loaded sounds. An area close to the primary auditory cortex in both species was activated more when emotionally positive sounds (playful barking, laughter) were played than when emotionally negative sounds (whining, crying) were played. This common response to emotion in dogs and humans was striking, and the researchers concluded that both species use similar brain mechanisms to process social information. These findings are not surprising when you consider that we 'share a similar social environment'.[1]

Dogs can suffer from emotional problems similar to those of people such as anxiety, depression, fears and phobias, anger, obsessions, compulsions and a broad range of stress-related problems. However, canine emotion is not complicated by irrational or rational thought. Human emotions are more complex because they have a greater capacity for imagining scenarios that sustain or exacerbate a negative emotion. We might think someone is talking about us when in reality the person might not have thought about us at all. Our minds do a great deal of story building that takes a toll on our emotions, whereas canine emotion is more like a young child's: raw, simple and truthful. Dogs in a multi-dog household, for example, might fight one minute and then be best friends the next – the fight has been forgotten and the dogs move on.

EMOTIONS AND BEHAVIOUR

It is undeniable that dogs' behaviour is directly influenced by their emotional experience. The same chemicals that drive human emotions also play a significant role in the emotional life of dogs.

Serotonin, for example, is a neurotransmitter that helps relay signals from one part of the brain to another. Serotonin is also found in the digestive tract and in blood platelets, and is responsible for regulating mood, appetite, sleep, memory, learning and social behaviour, and inhibiting aggressive response. Dopamine is a neurotransmitter that controls the brain's reward and pleasure centres, helping to focus attention and promote feelings of satisfaction. If a dog lacks the right balance of these important neurotransmitters, she can become depressed, irritable, impulsive, overreactive, anxious and more sensitive to pain.

EMOTIONS AND THE SENSES

Smell bypasses other parts of the brain and goes directly to the amygdala, the brain's emotional centre, in both dogs and humans; this is why a particular smell can evoke a positive or negative memory. Now think of how sensitive and powerful a dog's sense of smell is (see How dogs smell, page 51) and how emotional memory drives canine behaviour. In fact, input from a dog's nose dominates her brain, which is built around the information she gets from scent, and as smell is so closely linked to emotional memory, a dog's emotional experience is likely to be even greater than ours. Truly powerful stuff! This is one reason why I use food not just to motivate dogs to learn but to change the way they feel. Even if your dog is stressed or anxious, a positive emotional experience can occur with the anticipation of and/or presentation of food, with its enticing, evocative aroma.

There are circuits in the dog's brain that encourage seeking or hunting behaviour and circuits that elicit the fear response. When you turn on your dog's seeker system, or encourage her to play a game in the presence of something she fears, by presenting her with a tasty treat or a toy filled with food, you can turn on her seeker system at the same time that you turn off her fear. As soon as your dog anticipates food, her brain starts firing, effectively turning on her seeking system, shutting off the fear and making her feel good. As I mentioned earlier, the anticipation of the food can be far more powerful than the actual eating of the food itself, as the seeker system is turned off while the dog is eating. That is why I might encourage a dog to concentrate on food or cue her to go find food in the presence of the fear stimulus and then give the food once the stimulus has passed.

DO DOGS GET JEALOUS?

When a dog guards resources and space, monopolizes a person's attention, or fights with 'siblings', she could be acting out of jealousy. Although this anthropomorphizes a dog's intent, the canine expression of jealousy certainly mirrors that of a human. This seems to explain canine behaviour that is pushy, resentful and competitive. It's very common for a dog to push itself between hugging partners or invade the space of another dog that is being stroked. In fact, the presence of human carers can cause fights between dogs that competitively vie for attention. In evolutionary terms, a dog benefits from getting attention from an individual who provides comfort or is a primary food source, as this boosts the dog's chance of survival. Humans can mitigate these jealousies by teaching their dogs to share objects, space and attention, and by giving each dog plenty of good experiences while in the other's presence. Feeding, walking and stroking dogs at the same time can help quell the instinct for competitive rivalry.

DO DOGS FEEL GUILTY?

The word 'guilt' is often used to explain the body language of a dog that has done something bad because the language that 'guilty' dogs use is so familiar: crouched posture, bowed head, averted gaze, lifted paw, slowly blinking eyes. However, scientists believe that these submissive signals are not guilt at all but a dog's way of appeasing a person's anger even if the dog has no idea what he has done and why the person is angry.[2] Appeasement language is an evolutionary strategy that has helped

APPEASEMENT: crouched posture, bowed head, averted gaze

dogs live more successfully with humans. Dogs use these signals to effectively change their person's behaviour and avoid punishment by softening a negative reaction. The smaller and more contrite a dog appears to be, the less likely he feels he will be to exacerbate his person's anger and receive punishment.

Human self-awareness is highly sophisticated and linked to reflective consciousness. A person must be self-aware to feel guilty and able to understand how his or her behaviour has affected others in the past and how it will affect others in the future. Whereas human culture teaches us to consciously feel guilty, shameful or embarrassed for things we have done, it is unlikely that dogs are truly aware of how their behaviour affects others.

Therefore, researchers believe that appeasement displays are not a dog's admission of guilt but are used during times of stress and fear. So even if your dog has chewed your favourite cushion and you realize she has done something wrong by the look she gives you before you have discovered what has actually happened, it is more likely that past experience has taught her to associate a particular action or behaviour with your anger than that she feels guilty.

ARE DOGS EMPATHETIC?

Empathy is the capacity to understand and share the feelings of others, and while dogs definitely do show behaviour that looks empathetic – nuzzling a person who is crying, for example – it is hard to prove that dogs are actually feeling what another individual is feeling. Dogs certainly show behaviour that appears to indicate sympathy – feelings of pity for another's sorrow or misfortune – and they have a natural ability to show consolation behaviour towards those in distress, commonly the victim of a fight or argument.

So while dogs may not be empathetic in the true sense of the word, they do show 'emotional contagion' – responding to the emotions of another without fully understanding what that individual is feeling. This is similar to a baby that cries in response to the cry of another baby or a person who yawns in response to another individual's yawn.

EMOTIONAL CONTAGION: yawning when others yawn

Having worked with dogs for so long and seen so many examples of dogs licking and pawing at someone who is in distress, I can't help thinking that the quietness, stillness and sadness shown by a dog comforting a person who is crying, nuzzling a sick child in the hospital or laying its head on the lap of an elderly person certainly looks like empathy.

TOP TIP

Sit in front of your dog and yawn. You may find your dog yawns too – a clear example of emotional contagion.

The more we understand the emotional experience of dogs, the more we can help them live successfully in our human world, because the similarities are undeniable – dogs have the same brain structures that produce emotions in humans, produce the same hormones and experience the same chemical changes that humans go through during emotional states.

CHAPTER 4

THE SENSING DOG

To truly understand how dogs perceive the world, it's crucial to first understand the overall canine sensory experience – from the almost otherworldly capabilities of their amazing sense of smell to their ears' powerful ability to hear.

Senses are closely linked to emotions, and emotions are the driving force behind most behaviour, so understanding a dog's sensory capabilities is fundamental to appreciating what the dog's experience of our domestic world is really like.

Using a dog's senses to help him learn and combat behavioural issues is called sensory education, and positive trainers harness this powerful tool to help encourage dogs to gain confidence and learn effectively.

HOW DOGS SMELL

Dogs live in a world dominated by their sense of smell. The part of the brain devoted to smell is called the olfactory cortex; a dog's is approximately 40 times bigger than a human's, even though a dog's brain is just one-tenth the size of a human brain.

Dogs have an average of 250 million scent receptors in their nose, while humans have approximately 5 million. And while we are better at detecting odours when the scent is very strong, dogs can detect odours at very low concentrations – in parts per trillion.

When a dog smells something either in the air or on the ground, he disrupts his normal breathing process to gather scent. He sniffs to retain more of the scent for identification. Mobile nostrils that move independently from each other gather scent from all directions. The cool, wet mucus on and inside a dog's nose traps scent molecules, which dissolve in the mucus and are pushed up through the nose by tiny hairs called cilia. The nostrils lead to a bony shelf-like structure where the scent is trapped, and information gathered by receptor cells is then sent to the olfactory bulbs and on to the brain for processing.

Dogs have what is known as a vomeronasal or Jacobson's organ, located above the hard palate of the mouth just behind the incisors, at the base of the nasal cavity. The information received through this organ goes straight to the limbic system, which regulates mood and drives emotions and memory. Because smell and memory are so closely linked, different smells can be used to change the way a dog feels, as long as the smell is paired with something that he likes. Food can therefore help nervous and anxious dogs overcome their fears. Other scents – such as synthetic dog-appeasing pheromone or lavender – can be used to help lessen anxiety by promoting feelings of calm.

Every person has a unique scent signature that is common to all parts of the body and doesn't readily dissolve in water or air, unless the water is boiling or the air is very hot. The majority of a human's scent signature comes from the highly fatty substance secreted by our sebaceous glands. The apocrine sweat glands located in areas such as the underarms, genitals, back of the neck and tummy are activated by our emotional state, making it easy for dogs to smell how we are feeling, supporting the theory that dogs can smell fear.

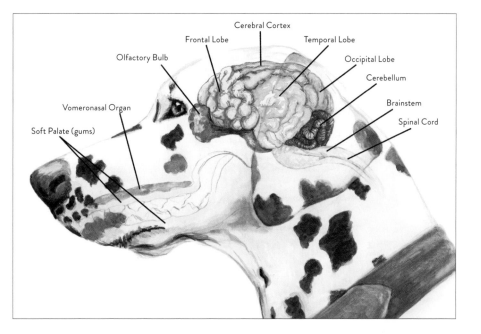

TOP TIP

You can use your dog's amazing scenting abilities to encourage learning by playing scent games such as hiding food and asking your dog to find it, as well as other scenting activities that will give him confidence and enrich his life.

Dogs can also detect scent by the skin cells (rafts) we shed in the process of living – about thirty thousand to forty thousand rafts a minute. Each time we move we leave a mass of skin cells and scent in our wake.

HOW DOGS SEE

Through the latest scientific research, we are beginning to learn more and more about how dogs see the world around them.

One of the biggest myths debunked by science is that dogs see only in black and white. Contrary to that popular belief, dogs have dichromatic vision, meaning that they can see shades of yellow and blue. To process these colours, the brain responds to and interprets neurons in the dog's retina. Blue light shades detected within the retina cause suppression of those neurons, and yellow light shades cause excitement of the neurons. The brain responds to

those signals with the colours we know as blue and yellow. In colour-blind people, the neurons have a neutral response to the colours red and green, so the brain interprets them as varying shades of grey. However, researchers have yet to determine whether that same phenomenon is true for dogs, or whether the brain assigns those colours in a different way.[1] So bear in mind that if you place a red toy on green grass, it may be a bit hard for your dog to find it!

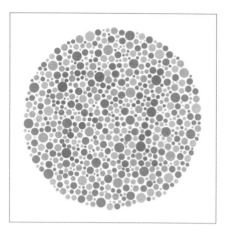

RED-GREEN COLOUR BLINDNESS: can you see the embedded number?

Another fascinating aspect of dogs' vision is their visual field of view, or peripheral vision. Whereas humans can see about 180 degrees around them, dogs can see up to 250 degrees. This field of vision varies by breed and is affected by how laterally directed the eyes are, but averages an impressive 60 to 70 degrees greater than the field of vision of humans.[2]

Have you ever wondered how well your dog can see in the dark? Dogs' sensitivity to light is another aspect of their vision that has been a topic of extensive scientific research. As dogs have evolved, so has their vision system. They are able to see quite well in low light, but have not lost their ability to see clearly in daylight as well. Dogs' minimum threshold of light needed for vision is significantly lower than that of humans, and it is believed they can see up to four times better than people can in low light.[3]

We typically judge human visual acuity (or the ability to see the details of an object without the object being blurred) using the Snellen fraction, with 20/20 being the base standard. For example, 20/40 means that the person needs to be 20 feet (6m) away to see object details that someone with 20/20 vision could see from 40 feet (12m) away. A dog's average visual acuity is thought to be somewhere around 20/75.[4]

The dog's visual system is fascinating. While it's not as highly developed in certain aspects compared to that of humans, it is designed to help them navigate the world according to their species-specific needs. Prey becomes an easier target at peak activity times such as dawn and dusk, so canine predators' vision needs to operate most efficiently during these periods of low light.

HOW DOGS TASTE THINGS

Knowing the extreme power of a dog's nose, one may assume that his sense of taste is equally powerful. Surprisingly, that isn't the case. Your dog's sense of taste isn't quite as impressive as his sense of smell; he has 1,700 papillae, or taste buds, compared to the 9,000 taste buds on a human tongue. Just as in humans, a dog's taste buds are replaced with new ones about every ten days.[5] The senses of taste and smell are closely linked and work together to keep your dog from ingesting potentially poisonous foods. However, domesticated dogs are vulnerable to human foods and medications that

have been artificially enhanced to taste better to humans, which encourages dogs to unknowingly eat things that pose a hazard to their health. Xylitol, for example, is widely used as a sugar substitute in foods like chewing gum, and while it is easily processed by the human body, it is highly toxic to dogs and can be fatal if treatment is not given.

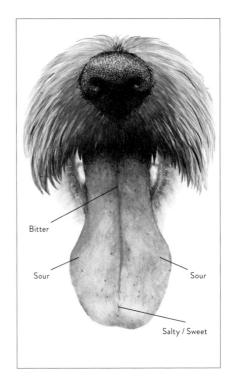

Like humans, dogs can pick up on sweet, salty, bitter and sour tastes. Dogs are one of the few mammals that can taste furaneol, a sweet flavour found in fruits. Dogs may have evolved this characteristic because in a natural diet they supplement their meat intake with available fruit as needed. Interestingly, domesticated cats do not have the same sensitivity to sweet and salty tastes that dogs do. It is believed that cats lack sensitivity to salt because they get the necessary sodium from their carnivorous diet.[6] Dogs do have less sensitivity to salt than humans, but have special taste receptors that are specifically programmed for meats and meat flavours. If you've ever wondered why your dog loves meat so much, just think about how finely tuned his sensory system is to seek it out!

TOP TIP

If your dog chews on inappropriate objects, spraying something bitter on the object may not stop him from chewing it. Your dog's taste receptors for bitterness are located on the back of the tongue, and he may miss the bitter taste entirely as he swallows.

Another fascinating fact about dogs' sense of taste is that they are particularly attuned to the taste of water, a sensory feature that humans lack. The taste receptor for water is located on the tip of a dog's tongue and becomes more sensitive to the taste after a particularly sugary or salty meal. This may have developed as an evolutionary response to keep dogs hydrated while eating a diet heavy in sodium-laden meats.[7]

HOW DOGS HEAR

You may have heard that dogs' hearing is much better than humans (hence the various whistles and dog-controlling sound devices). While the human ear can detect pitches up to only 20,000 hertz, dogs can hear frequencies up to about 45,000 hertz. What is even more fascinating than the stark differences

in hearing between humans and dogs is how they made that discovery in the first place. To measure the frequency to which dogs can hear, researchers taught dogs to respond to a presented sound by selecting between two actions. Typically the dogs would choose between two bowls where a reward would be dispensed; they had to choose the bowl on the same side in which the sound was heard. If the dog chose incorrectly, the reward would not be dispensed. The researchers tested the dogs at varying frequencies and intensities to determine what the dogs could hear and what they couldn't.[8]

Dogs are not born with the ability to hear. In fact, they are born deaf. Within about a month, though, puppies have developed exceptional hearing and are able to pick up sounds from all directions. Once fully established, dogs' sensitivity to sound is so acute that they have been shown to be able to detect tiny changes of pitch between notes. With such a keen sense of hearing, it's no wonder that some dogs prefer to leave the room at the sound of a vacuum cleaner or a baby's cries.

Certain dogs are more sensitive to sound than others. The inclination to sound sensitivity may vary by breed: certain breeds have evolved over time to rely on sound to do a job such as the Border collie being able to hear the farmers' calls or whistles over long distances while herding sheep. Because some dogs are unable to filter between active listening – that is, the act of focusing one's hearing on a specific sound – and passive hearing, when there is a noise in the background that the brain hears but doesn't actively listen to, these dogs can develop sound sensitivity or noise phobias. Research also indicates that dogs with sound sensitivity are more prone to anxious behaviours. In a 2015 study, the dogs that were the most fearful of noises were also more likely to exhibit separation anxiety and fearfulness in new situations, and they took longer to recover from a stressful event than the dogs that were less noise phobic.[9]

Interestingly, studies have shown that puppies that are desensitized to noises like thunderstorms, fireworks and the sounds of the city are less likely to develop noise phobias as adults. This same sort of sensory education can be used when working with dogs that have already developed noise phobias.

WHAT TOUCH MEANS TO DOGS

Perhaps one reason we bond so closely with our dogs is that we see so many of our behaviours and mannerisms mirrored in theirs. Dogs, like humans, begin exploring their sense of touch from the moment they're born.

A puppy's mother will lick and nuzzle him, both as a comforting gesture and to stimulate the pup to eliminate waste. In turn, puppies must rely on touch in order to nurse and to seek comfort in the warmth of their mother and siblings. These reciprocated forms of touch can help establish a bond between mother and pups, a bond that is critical to the pups' survival at such a young age. As a result, puppies can become visibly distraught when separated from their mother or their siblings.[10] These social attachments with mother and siblings are a critical part of the puppy's early socialization, and they can be transferred to humans to help the pup form social attachments as he ages. Puppies should never be removed from their mother or littermates before they are at least seven to eight weeks old. Doing so earlier can damage the pup's

ability to learn and form healthy social attachments with other dogs as he grows. The pup's mother and littermates provide valuable feedback for all sorts of social skills needed in later life such as play, feeding and sleeping.

Some dogs are more sensitive to touch than others. Dogs that are experiencing pain or inflammation may be sensitive in those areas, and some dogs have naturally sensitive paws.

If puppies are not conditioned from a young age to understand that an approaching human hand is not threatening, they may grow up to fear the touch of humans. Many puppies have an automatic defensive reflex when they see a hand coming towards them, so habituating a pup to touch from an early age (birth to 16 weeks old) is typically recommended.

Another fascinating component of your dog's sense of touch are his sensitive facial whiskers. Whereas humans feel the world through their fingers, dogs often use their face. These whiskers, called vibrissae, are located above the eyes, on the muzzle and below the jaw on the sides of the muzzle. Vibrissae are present in nearly all mammals, with the exception of humans. The fact that they are so common across species suggests their significance for an animal's safety and survival.[11] The vibrissae are loaded with nerves that send sensory signals to the brain about nearby objects, helping to compensate for their imperfect vision.

Touch sensitivities vary from dog to dog, but you should always use particular care when touching the head, muzzle, tail, abdomen and paws. Nerve endings along the dog's spine and towards the tail make the back a particularly sensitive area, albeit one where most dogs like to be touched. Foot sensitivity is probably why so many dogs hate having their paws touched

TOP TIP

Don't trim your dog's whiskers! As we learn more about a dog's sensory experience, we are finding out just how important they are to dogs' spatial awareness and sensory abilities.

or nails clipped. Some dogs also suffer from a skin sensitivity condition known as hyperalgesia, making any kind of handling or grooming very painful. If your dog reacts negatively while being handled or brushed, take him to the veterinarian to rule out a medical cause.

Dogs' senses are tailored to meet their specific needs and vary depending on what breed or mix of breeds they are. Dogs that are used to doing specific tasks will often have one or more dominant senses, depending on how they have been taught and the job they have been bred to do. Even companion dogs can benefit from having their senses stimulated by doing a specific task or activity such as a dog sport or being taken for a walk. Encouraging your dog to use specific senses provides important enrichment and benefits both physical and mental health.

Habituating a pup to being touched from birth is extremely important. Habituation helps to reduce a negative response to a stimulus after repeated presentations, as the puppy or dog learns to tolerate and even enjoy being handled or touched. Habituation needs to be done slowly so as not to overwhelm the pup and cause a negative association with the stimulus or experience.

PART II

THE SECRET MEANINGS OF BODY AND VOCAL LANGUAGE

The subtleties of canine language can be easily missed or misunderstood, and it's up to those of us who work with dogs on a regular basis to study this language and be their translators. Because dogs have evolved so closely with humans, most people who share their lives with them have developed an incredible ability to communicate across species. However, there is a rich secret language that is only just being discovered, and research results are shining more light on just how incredible our dogs are.

CHAPTER 5

LATERAL LANGUAGE

You might be surprised to learn that the way your dog wags her tail, smells an object or manipulates a toy is linked to her emotional state. Lateral bias is apparent when a human or animal shows a preference for one side of their body over the other, which is linked to the primary use of the left or right brain hemisphere.

PAW PREFERENCE

Just as humans favour one hand (and arm, leg and foot) over the other, dogs tend to have a bias when it comes to using their paws. Watch your dog play with a toy and see if she favours a certain paw. This is called paw preference. Most dogs favour using one paw over the other, but a minority show dexterity with both (called ambilateral in dogs), just like a person who is ambidextrous.

Evidence suggests that paw preference and the strength of that preference are closely linked with emotions and behaviour. Dogs that favour the left paw more often use the right hemisphere of their brain, while right-pawed dogs have a more active left hemisphere, and this difference is reflected in their behavioural tendencies. These findings aren't surprising, considering that the right brain hemisphere controls the left side of the body and the left hemisphere controls the right side of the body. The left hemisphere is activated when the brain is processing positive emotion such as happiness, excitement, attention and affection as well as something familiar; the right hemisphere takes over when the brain processes sadness, fear and other negative emotions.

LEFT-PAWED: higher arousal (right hemisphere)

RIGHT-PAWED: lower arousal (left hemisphere)

LEFT TAIL WAG: cautious (right hemisphere)

RIGHT TAIL WAG: confident (left hemisphere)

Various studies have shown that right-pawed dogs are less easily aroused and are better able to cope with novel environments and situations, whereas left-pawed dogs show more stranger-directed aggression than right-pawed or ambilateral dogs.[1] Other studies have shown that dogs with no paw preference were more reactive to loud noises, whereas dogs with a strong paw preference were more confident and playful and less anxious or impulsive than dogs with weaker paw preferences.[2]

Interestingly, hand preference could also be linked to learning and emotional issues in people. Approximately 85 per cent of people are right-handed, and a preference for using one hand over the other is noticeable in children by about 18 months of age. Right-handed bias could have evolved because natural selection produced a majority of people with speech and language control in the left brain hemisphere. Because the left hemisphere also controls the movements of the right hand, evolutionary development produced a majority of individuals with a left hemisphere speech/language bias and a right-handed preference to produce written language.[3]

DECODING THE WAG

Does your dog wag her tail more to the right or the left? The sweep and direction of the tail wag is an outwards expression of emotion and reflects the way the two sides of the brain process information. Studies have shown that dogs wag their tails more to the right when greeting people they know and like as well as unfamiliar people (if they are social dogs), although the tail wags lower. They wag their tails more to the left when seeing an unfamiliar dog.[4] Again, the right tail wag is controlled by the left brain hemisphere, which is associated with more confident behaviours, while the left wag is controlled by the right brain hemisphere, associated with more cautious approach behaviours.

HEAD TURNING

The way your dog turns his head might also be an indicator of how he feels. Researchers simultaneously presented dogs with identical stimuli on both their left and right sides while eating from a bowl. The direction in which they turned their heads indicated which side of the brain was involved in processing and responding to the stimulus, revealing the dogs' emotional reaction to it.[5] Dogs turned consistently to the right in response to the social cues of canine isolation or disturbance calls and canine play vocalizations, but turned to the left when they heard thunder.

Dogs also turned their heads left in response to images of cats and snakes but not to images of other dogs. With repeated exposure, there was a change to the right, indicating that the left side of the brain and its associated positive emotions were involved. This suggests that novel experiences may influence fear and other negative emotions that tend to be processed by the right side of the brain.[6]

The way a dog tilts or cocks her head to one side when you talk to her could also be linked to how she feels or reacts in a certain situation, but it's more likely that she's trying to work out what you're saying rather than having an emotional reaction to how you're saying it. I believe it's the canine way of saying 'Huh?' or 'What are you talking about?' Some researchers believe that because a number of dogs have long noses the head tilt helps them see better, but I read it as more of a signal that is used when a dog is trying to hear and understand you better. Human language is very confusing!

NOSE BIAS

While paw preference and tail wagging are controlled by opposite hemispheres in the brain, what goes in the right nostril is processed on the right side of the brain, and what goes in the left nostril goes to the left side.[7]

Researchers have recently discovered that when dogs investigate different scents, they tend to begin and continue investigating 'negative' odours (such as adrenaline and the smell of a veterinarian) with their right nostril, but begin with the right and switch to the left nostril when investigating 'positive' smells like food or the odour of a familiar dog. Appreciating nose bias is beneficial to everyone who has a dog but is particularly important if a dog is nervous or anxious. Presenting a dog's favourite food to her in the presence of something she fears but at a sufficiently safe distance, can completely change the way her brain works and therefore how she perceives that stimulus. This underscores why using food to encourage learning and to help dogs overcome fears is so beneficial – a good smell can promote positive feelings!

Knowing your dog's bias not only will make teaching her easier (if your dog is having trouble doing a task that involves using a paw she doesn't usually use, you can encourage her to switch to using the paw that is easier), but also allows you to better understand her emotional state and find ways to reduce any stress she may be experiencing. You can also better understand the way she responds to you – and hopefully her tail wags more to the right when she welcomes you home at the end of the day!

CHAPTER 6

THE LANGUAGE OF SOCIALIZATION

What a joy it is to see a dog that is relaxed and friendly! The body is fluid, the tail is loose and the legs are relaxed. The face is soft, eyes slightly squinting and the lower jaw hangs open with the tongue resting loosely in the mouth. The body position is neutral, neither braced forwards nor leaning back.

Happy dogs display a confidence and friendliness: they encourage and at times actively seek contact from other dogs or people. They enjoy social interaction and feel comfortable in their environment.

Socially confident dogs are good at giving passive signals that serve to reduce the chance of undesired attention and to encourage social interaction, as well as being good at more active signals such as play bows to encourage friendly and non-threatening interaction.

TAIL WAGGING

Tail wagging is a frequently misinterpreted signal. Most people believe that a dog will wag her tail only when she is happy, but dogs also wag their tails when aroused, overly stimulated or frustrated. The tail wag is a social signal, reflecting what the dog is thinking and feeling, and the way the tail moves indicates whether the dog is friendly, insecure, fearful, aroused, challenged or warning you to stay away. A change in tail position indicates a change in thought and intention.

You can usually tell what your dog is feeling by looking at one part while watching what the rest of her body is doing. The way her tail is positioned reflects what she is feeling, but it's important to note that different breeds hold their tails in different ways. A resting beagle might hold her tail relatively high, whereas a whippet's natural tail position is low and curved.

In general:

- A confident or aroused dog will hold her tail in the air, allowing scent from the anal glands to circulate more freely and advertise her presence.
- A tail that wags around and around like a helicopter and is accompanied by relaxed fluid body movement and a wiggling bottom signals friendliness and a willingness to engage.

Because the tail is a prime indicator of mood as well as being important for balance and signalling, dogs with docked tails have a harder time using their tails to communicate effectively, so that vital communicative signals can be missed. A long moving tail is easily seen and interpreted, whereas a short tail is hard to read.

TAIL IN THE AIR: confident or aroused

THE LANGUAGE OF TAILS

CONFIDENT TAIL

EXCITED 'HELICOPTER' TAIL

RELAXED TAIL

RELAXED TAIL WAG

PLAY

APPROPRIATE PLAY: a puppy's play behaviour promotes social ease

Dog-to-dog play includes active and repetitive behaviours that mean different things when performed in different contexts, but in general, play helps dogs gain experience and develop important life skills that promote good physical and mental health. Play can be something of a mock battle in which dogs rehearse physical actions they might need in life, and good play is all about winning and losing the game by 'self-handicapping'. It's all about give-and-take: being able to roll over as the other dog dives on top and then to reverse the situation, and keeping the play roles equal.

Successful, fulfilling play requires a dog to accurately read vocal and body signals. Dogs that don't get the opportunity to play usually have trouble communicating and identifying these signals. Dogs that play rudely – body slamming, mouthing too hard, mounting and generally causing mayhem – can provoke negative reactions in other dogs.

PLAY BOW: peaceful intentions/inviting play

Play begins in puppyhood and helps puppies develop good coordination while allowing them to practise a series of exaggerated behaviours that promote social ease. Most young dogs learn how to play well from their peers or their elders, but socially inexperienced or rude dogs can cause problems. If your dog is pushy or plays too rough, he should not interact with other dogs until he learns to greet and play nicely.

Appropriate play sometimes looks very rough, but human intervention is usually not needed. Conflict is avoided as long as each dog allows the other to win *and* lose the game, but as dogs become more aroused, a mock battle can turn into something more serious.

Most dogs play safely with each other by relying on a series of cut-off signals that communicate their peaceful intentions. They use play bows and displacement behaviours such as sniffing, sneezing, yawning, itching and licking for brief moments throughout play to communicate that any future action is still playful.

TOP TIP

Teach your dog a reliable cue and use it to call your dog back to you before play gets too rowdy. This will give her time to calm down before playing again.

The beauty of play is that most dogs want to keep playing with others right into adulthood. Play works well when both dogs know the rules, maintain a low level of arousal, and are willing to win and lose the game. Play can become quite vocal; this is usually OK unless vocalizations increase and/or one dog is giving appeasement signals and trying to get away. If the other dog recognizes these signals and backs off, there is a good understanding between players, but if the other dog ignores the signals, usually humans will need to intervene. By understanding how dogs play, you can help ensure that play remains a fun and healthy activity for everyone.

GREETING BEHAVIOUR

You may have noticed that dogs greet each other in an arc – a ritualized greeting pattern that starts when two dogs approach each other, touch noses, and sniff first each other's mouths and then around the genital area. Every dog has a unique scent signature, and it is thought that dogs can tell another's age, gender, health, sexual availability and emotional state through pheromones released in urine and by glands located in these areas. This is also why some dogs have an embarrassing habit of smelling a human's crotch, especially with strangers or people they meet less often. Apocrine glands located in the crotch area also give dogs a lot of information about the person they smell, which is good for the dog but not so comfortable for the human.

SNIFFING ARC: greeting hello

MOUNTING

Unless a female is in oestrus, mounting or humping behaviour has more to do with social dominance than with sex. Puppies will mount other pups from an early age, long before they reach puberty, as they test out their flexibility and control on their more submissive brothers and sisters.

Social dominance is important to both males and females, which is why both genders use mounting behaviour with other dogs and sometimes with people. As I have said before, even though social dominance is important in the canine world, dogs do not come into our homes with a well-thought-out plan to take over. When dogs mount people, it may be because they are overexcited, feel uncomfortable with a person's presence or simply want to control movement. Mounting is a good way to control an individual in the dog's environment, especially if that individual is unwelcome or unknown to the dog.

Dogs will also mount each other during play. This is usually not an aggressive act (unless the mounter is trying to bully and the dog being mounted takes umbrage) but a good rehearsal for future sexual or dominant behaviour and actually helps make aggression less likely.

Mounting behaviour can lessen once the sex organs are removed, because the removal of sex hormones tends to lessen reactivity, but neutering and spaying alone cannot be relied on to fix a humping problem. In fact, while the desire to control others might diminish in some dogs, neutering can make others less confident and more reactive, therefore increasing the desire to control by mounting.

While it can be frustrating to deal with your dog's mounting habit, bear in mind the cause may be as harmless as the dog wanting attention or wanting to control a sibling or play pal that has something your dog wants. Mounting is a great way for a dog to get attention and provide a distraction, and it can be an effective strategy to steal a toy from the dog being mounted.

SCENT MARKING

SCENT MARKING: information communication/ marking territory

Marking territory with urine and faeces is just one way that dogs leave information about themselves and gather information about others that have gone before. Smelling another dog's scent is an effective way to get information without actually meeting, so it's important to allow your dog time to put his nose to the ground rather than pulling him away.

Male dogs will usually lift their legs on vertical surfaces such as trees or lampposts to get their scent as high as possible. This is useful as it not only puts scent at nose height, making it easier for another dog to smell, but allows the scent molecules to disperse over a wider area and shows the sniffer how big the marker is. Marking vertical surfaces also makes it harder for other dogs to mark over it. Some smaller male and female dogs go to special lengths to get their urine higher, doing handstands against a vertical surface such as a wall or spraying urine as they are walking. Female dogs will also mark territory by releasing urine, and both genders have a tendency to scrape the surrounding area with their back paws after toileting, which not only deposits scent from the paws onto the ground but again lifts the scent into the air to disperse it over a wider area. These chemical messages are the equivalent of writing a note or reading the daily local news.

Dogs, like cats, also mark places, objects and even people by rubbing their faces and bodies on them. Spreading scent tells others that they have prior claim to a particular object or area, but it can also be a signal that a dog is uncomfortable with a person's presence.

LICKING

Licking is important from the day a dog is born. Mothers will lick their pups immediately after birth to stimulate breathing, facilitate movement and encourage their pups to eliminate waste. Without this licking, puppies would have little hope of surviving. Pups also learn that licking around their mother's mouth will stimulate her to regurgitate food for them, although this is less common in domestic litters. Licking is also an important appeasement signal used during greeting rituals, and you will often see puppies licking around their mother's mouth as a gesture of submission. Pups and adult dogs often repeat these behaviours with more dominant dogs as well as their human carers.

If a dog is wounded, she will usually lick the wound to clean it and ease the pain. In fact, some dogs will lick parts of their body that are painful even if no

LICKING: submission/attention/appeasement

wound is present. Although the licking action helps clean debris out of a wound, and saliva does have some healing properties, it also carries bacteria that can cause infection if the wound is not properly treated. Dogs with allergies or yeast infections will often lick moist areas such as the genitals or the paws to relieve itching, pain and sensitivity.

THE ZOOMIES

Does your dog ever run around like a crazed animal? One moment she is still and relaxed, the next she's darting around your home like a rocket. The canine zoomies, better known as frenetic random activity periods or FRAPs, help pups release energy. FRAPs tend to happen during play between dogs and/ or people and times of great excitement. Some dogs will zoom after being groomed or bathed, maybe as a way to release built-up tension from an activity they dislike. Whatever the cause of your dog's zoomies, it's a normal, harmless behaviour; the dog releases that pent-up energy and pet parents smile.

TOP TIPS

Before you start teaching your dog, simply play with her or be part of her favourite activity. This encourages bonding and shows your dog that you are the source of fun. And when it comes to teaching your dog cues, make sure you use humane, fear-free techniques that promote confidence and encourage learning.

- You should start socializing your dog as soon as she joins your family. Socialization promotes security and confidence, and dogs that are socially confident feel less need to be aggressive towards people and other animals.

- Give your dog plenty of exercise. Exercise is a powerful stress reliever and helps prevent or modify behaviours such as excessive barking and chewing or stress-related behaviours such as separation anxiety and aggression.

- Exercise your dog's brain. Using activity toys and playing with your dog provides important mental stimulation and increases the human/animal bond.

- Stay healthy – both of you! You are what you eat, and so is your dog. Your dog's behaviour can be greatly influenced by the food she eats. Avoid cheap brands, and feed your dog a good, healthy diet.

CHAPTER 7

THE LANGUAGE OF FEAR

All canine language communicates intent and is used to influence behaviour in others, either to draw them in for social contact or to keep them away. Although it is relatively easy to read the language of a fearful dog, there are some signals that are either misunderstood or hard to interpret because they are so subtle.

Fear is the dog's response to a perceived external threat and is handled by the amygdala, the brain's emotional centre; anxiety is the dog's response to an anticipated (as yet unseen) threat and is handled by the prefrontal cortex.[1] The presence of a stranger may elicit a fear response because that person is unfamiliar. A dog may also be anxious in a known person's presence because he has had a negative experience and anticipates that something similar might happen again.

Although some dogs are genetically predisposed to be fearful, an abnormal susceptibility to fear often stems from a single traumatic incident or from prolonged exposure to a fearful stimulus. Dogs that have had limited experience with people, other dogs or different situations can also be fearful in social situations and actively avoid social interaction.

Appeasement or deference language is designed to appease others. It is usually the first line of defence when a dog is either nervous about someone approaching or in an overwhelming or scary environment. Healthy relationships between dogs are maintained by deference language to keep the peace and avoid physical violence, which is important for group survival. While active appeasement language like muzzle licking communicates that the dog wants attention – it is often seen during greetings – passive, submissive behaviours like tummy flips communicate that the dog does not want attention and indeed wants that individual to go away (see facing page.)

Some examples of appeasement and deference language include the following:

- Head bobbing or lowering
- Muzzle licking
- Head turning
- Whale eye (showing the whites)
- Flat ears
- Lip licking
- Lifting paw
- Low tail carriage
- Wagging tail

- Tail tucked between the legs
- Curved and crouched body
- Tummy flip – the dog flips over quickly, exposing his tummy; he is not asking for a tummy rub but is withdrawing from interaction
- Play bows
- Submissive urination

A tail held low or between the legs signals a lack of confidence, nervousness, submission or fear (see facing page); a tail held high but wagged more slowly means the dog is cautious and assessing a situation.

Dogs usually use a slight tail wag during greetings, as the dog is cautiously assessing risk; a slow, low tail wag usually indicates insecurity.

THE LANGUAGE OF APPEASEMENT AND SUBMISSION

TUMMY FLIP: leave me alone

WHALE EYE: deference

TUCKED TAIL: lack of confidence

Displacement language is used when the dog is anxious or stressed and needs to calm himself or to divert a perceived threat's attention. This language is typically active and includes the following:

- Sneezing
- Shaking
- Sniffing
- Nose licking
- Yawning

- Spinning
- Pacing
- Chattering teeth
- Shaking off – a release of stress and tension

Stress and fear language is used when the dog is experiencing a heightened fear response: it consists of passive and active signalling that communicates intention. Most fearful dogs use this language to keep the thing they fear away rather than having to fight it off, but if the stimulus keeps approaching, the dog is left with no other option but to run away or to fight for survival.

It is often assumed that yawning dogs are tired. While this may be true in some instances, yawning is also a sign of stress. Other signs include the following:

- Lip licking or tongue flicking
- Micro body freezing – the dog is still for a few seconds before reacting
- Body freezing – the dog freezes until the threat goes away or he decides to use fight or flight
- Low tail carriage – indicates discomfort and uncertainty
- Whale eye – the dog turns his head away but keeps looking at the perceived threat, showing the whites of his eyes
- Head turn – away from a threat

- Furrowed brow, curved eyebrows – caused by facial tension
- Tense jaw – the mouth is closed, and the dog is preparing for action
- Curved tongue – the tongue is curved at the edges from tension
- Raspy 'dry' panting – nervousness reduces saliva production
- Shaking – a release of adrenaline causes the dog to shake himself as if trying to get water off his coat

THE LANGUAGE OF DISPLACEMENT AND STRESS

SPINNING: calming himself

COWERING BODY, LOW TAIL CARRIAGE: stress and fear

SEPARATION DISTRESS

Dogs that fear being alone should never be reprimanded or put in their place for trying to deal with that fear by vocalizing or being destructive. Because dogs form such strong social attachments with their human carers, it can be terrifying when that person goes away. In her incredible book *Animals in Translation*, Temple Grandin writes how separation distress is linked to the most primitive systems of the brain, including those for pain response, place attachment and thermoregulation (the regulation of body temperature). When we are separated from people we love, we often talk about the pain we feel and the desire to be home. We talk about friendly people as being warm and unfriendly people as being cold. Researchers believe that 'social warmth evolved out of the brain system that handles physical warmth' and

that 'social attachment is a survival mechanism that evolved partly from the survival mechanism of keeping the body warm'.[2] I can certainly relate to that. While I was filming my TV show *It's Me or the Dog*, I spent a good deal of time away from my family, including my five-year-old daughter, and the pain of being parted from her for so long was so intense that I became depressed and physically ill. My experience taught me that among other things, the fear that dogs experience can be debilitating and should never be trivialized. It also taught me that, far from what other behaviour experts believe, physically comforting a fearful dog doesn't reinforce his fear. In fact, the secure attachment provided by a trusted individual helps calm anxiety and promotes confidence, just as a mother does when she comforts her scared child.

FIGHTING FEAR

Fearful dogs can be rehabilitated, but success depends on the type of fear, the duration of exposure and how adaptable the dog is to learning. Dogs that have phobias such as fear of noise can be harder to treat because the phobia is usually deeply ingrained. But with time, understanding, patience and a good rehabilitation plan, you can turn a fearful dog's life around.

The key to successful rehabilitation is the close link between fear and curiosity. A dog may be fearful of a particular situation, but as long as his brain is not shut down with so many negative emotions that he is truly incapable of learning, you can engage him by using his natural curiosity. You can do this by presenting him with something powerful that he loves at a safe distance from the source of his fear, and as the dog gains confidence, gradually decreasing that distance. Turning on the dog's thinking brain deactivates the emotional brain. This enhances the dog's attention with positive motivation and allows him to move into a calmer state where learning can take place. For example, if your dog fears people who pass him on the street, you can present a person (ask a good friend to help) at a safe distance, engage your dog's thinking brain with an activity such as a game of tug or 'go find the treat', and play the game as your friend walks past. This not only turns a negative experience into a positive one but it also starts building a positive association between the person and the game. If these combined experiences continue, the sight of a person will give your dog positive emotions as he anticipates the start of the game. The game is even more powerful if it's something your dog loves to do and is played only in the presence of people or another stimulus that your dog fears.

GIVE BACK CONTROL

Fear can be quite debilitating for dogs because, unlike people, dogs have no control over their fear. In general, people have more power to deal with their fear in that they can manage it by changing their situation and environment or by getting help with therapy or medication. Dogs don't have that power. If they are fearful of something they can indeed run away, but they can't if they're confined in a home or restricted by a lead that you hold. They can fight, but this is not acceptable in our society and they are punished, shut away or abandoned in shelters. Giving dogs the power to cope with their fears as well as guiding the choices they make can go a long way towards helping them become more confident.

If your dog is fearful of new people coming into your home but is not aggressive towards them, give him the power to deal with the situation in the best way he knows how. Observe how your dog reacts when a stranger enters your home. If he slinks away and avoids the person, let him! Practising avoidance is one of the best ways a dog can cope with a situation, so if he retreats into another room or goes to his bed, allow him to do so. You can also help the situation by asking your new guest to refrain from approaching, talking to or touching your dog. When any attempt at social interaction is removed, this takes pressure off the dog, giving him the space he needs to be comfortable. If your dog prefers not to socialize, respect his decision and don't force the issue – not all dogs are social butterflies.

If your dog barks at guests as they come in, and you worry that the situation might escalate into something worse if your guest attempts to make contact, relieve the pressure on your dog by putting him behind a baby gate or in his own room while the guest is there. Creating a safe zone for your dog to go to when new people come into the house is a great way to keep everyone safe and give you (and your dog) peace of mind.

Allowing your dog some autonomy while providing a guiding hand will give your dog confidence and the power to cope with a world over which he has no control. Adapting your dog's environment and helping him to get accustomed to whatever has caused the fear in the past will help overcome what can be an overwhelming and debilitating emotion. Observing and understanding what your dog is saying physically and vocally, even when the language is very subtle, can help you address his needs, improve his confidence and reduce his fear.

CHAPTER 8

THE LANGUAGE OF AGGRESSION

Aggressive behaviour indicates a dog's need to increase distance from a perceived danger. A dog's threat-and-action displays range from a subtle lip lift to a deep bite. In most cases the dog's intention is not to do harm but to make the threat go away. We can easily read aggressive language such as lunging, growling, snapping, barking and biting, but some other warning signals can be hard to see or easily misunderstood. For example, a yawning dog might be tired, but he could also be yawning because he's stressed in a particular situation. If a person misunderstands the context of the yawn, they could be at risk of being bitten.

Dogs can bite when they are fearful, nervous, anxious, frustrated or in pain, but they are also more likely to bite if they have high prey drive, which leads to biting and/or killing of another animal as part of the predatory sequence. Aggressive behaviour sometimes arises from a combination of hidden problems that are deeply ingrained. Think of the behaviour as a weedy plant you can see and touch that is being sustained by a complex system of underground roots. If you can get to the root system and eliminate each one, the weed will die, but if you just cut off the stem and leaves, this often stimulates the weed to grow more actively. Similarly, if you use punitive training methods to suppress your dog's aggressive behaviour, these methods not only don't address the root cause but can act as a stimulant, sustaining stress and keeping the behaviour alive.

Aggressive behaviour in all dogs, large and small, needs to be handled sensitively and with compassion because aggressive dogs are under stress, and this stress needs to be managed while a behavioural modification plan is put into place. Every case is unique, so every treatment plan is different.

Dogs use defensive language to warn a perceived threat to back away. They use offensive language when they feel they have no other option but to respond with violence. This language is usually easy to see – however, signals like micro freezes (where the dog goes still for a brief moment before lashing out) are harder to interpret. Aggressive signals include the following, in typical order of escalation:

- Hard, staring eyes
- Tense mouth
- Micro freeze
- Lips pushed forwards, teeth exposed as the dog growls
- Ears pricked and held in a V shape
- Creased forehead
- Low sustained growl

Threatening/arousal signals include the following:

- Body stiff and leaning forwards
- Raised hackles
- Wagging tail
- Low sustained growl or barking
- Tail held between the legs or high over the back with tail hair puffed out
- Tail extended and curved, signalling the dog is tense and ready to take offensive or defensive action

A wagging tail does not always indicate a happy dog. Dogs that are overly aroused often wag their tails very fast. A dog that is wagging his tail but barking with a defensive body posture, tense face and hard, staring eyes is overly aroused and frustrated, which means that he should not be approached.

THE LANGUAGE OF AGGRESSION

DEFENSIVE/THREATENING: hard, staring eyes, tense mouth, micro freeze, pricked ears, creased forehead, body stiff, leaning forwards

AGGRESSIVE: growl with teeth exposed

THREATENING: raised hackles

THE LANGUAGE OF AGGRESSION

THREATENING: tail held high over the back with tail hair puffed out

AIR SNAPPING: a warning to back away

OVERT AGGRESSION: lunging to bite

Escalating signals include the following:

- Air snapping – used to warn something to back away
- Snapping with skin contact but no damage
- Biting with skin contact that bruises
- Biting that breaks skin
- Biting that breaks and tears skin
- Biting that breaks and tears skin; dog holds on and shakes

SUPPRESSING AGGRESSIVE BEHAVIOUR

Suppressing aggressive behaviour is very different from actually changing it. Anyone can use hard physical or mental punishment to suppress negative behaviour, and though suppression works quickly, the repercussions render any momentary 'successes' useless, particularly in the long term. Physical or mental suppression causes an aggressive dog more stress, even when it appears the behaviour has stopped and the dog is no longer reacting. What is seen as calmer behaviour, so often exhibited by dogs whose behaviour has been suppressed by violent means, is mistakenly labelled 'calm submission', but in reality it hides an internal physical and mental struggle. After violence, dogs resort to physical stillness because it is more likely to stop an aggressor. So although the suppressed dog may appear to be calmer – he lies still, pants with an open mouth or keeps his mouth firmly closed, stares in front of him, and lets his body go loose – he is not truly calm, because it takes a long time for cortisol, the stress hormone, to leave the body after a stress-inducing event. A dog that is truly calm breathes at a steady pace and has a regular heartbeat as well as has a relaxed, fluid body, gentle eyes and little facial tension.

WHY DOGS GUARD THEIR RESOURCES

Protecting things that are valuable to us is normal and expected. We alarm our homes and cars, hold our families and possessions close to us, and get angry when someone violates our space and takes things we value. Our dogs also protect things that are important to them, yet when they try to defend their territory or guard resources, they are punished.

If someone tried to steal your bag from you, what would you do? Would you try to take it back or would you let it go? Chances are you might react on impulse to protect a valued resource, but either decision could compromise your safety. Dogs do the same thing when something of value is taken away from them. They might let you take it, or they might warn you to stay away by lifting a lip, exposing their teeth, keeping very still, growling, snapping or biting if you don't pay heed to their warning language.

Even though guarding behaviour is normal, it becomes a problem when it occurs in our homes, especially if the dog has bitten. The best way to persuade a dog to stop guarding a resource (this could be food, toys, furniture, dog beds or even people) is to prevent the behaviour from happening in the first place by teaching your dog to share the things he values rather than guarding them. Punishing your dog for resource guarding will make him more insecure, but the more you show him that you are the source of all his good things and that your presence around what he values means that good things happen to him, the more confident he will be and the less he will feel the need to guard.

TOP TIP

If your dog's guarding behaviour concerns you, remove the object or block off the location he is guarding so he can't keep practising the behaviour. Then call in a qualified trainer to help solve the problem, as this is a serious behaviour that needs professional attention.[1]

PREVENTING DOG BITES

If your dog has bitten a person or another dog, it's vital that you determine what caused the bite and control future situations so that your dog is never in a position where he can bite again. Whether your dog has bitten once or has a history of biting, your number one priority is to keep your dog comfortable and other people and animals safe by managing your dog's environment at all times. It's hard to supervise a dog's interactions all the time and virtually impossible to prevent encounters between your dog and people and other animals, so you must be ready to deal with this. All dog owners know that people will approach and touch their dogs without asking. It's understandable, because we live in a country of dog lovers, but there must be boundaries as well as clear information on how to greet a dog appropriately.

Basic rules should be followed such as these: avoid kissing dogs on the nose; do not hug a strange dog or a dog that you do not know very well; do not reach out to touch a dog uninvited; watch out for signals that a dog is uncomfortable such as avoidance, lip licking and yawning; and if you're told it's OK to pet a dog, allow him to come into your personal space rather than invading his. Building general awareness of these respectful practices keeps everyone safe and comfortable.

Raising dogs in a loving environment as well as handling and training them humanely will give them confidence to cope with the new and unfamiliar both at home and out and about. Socializing your dog well will make him feel more comfortable in all kinds of situations and encourage sociability rather than social awkwardness.

CHAPTER 9

THE LANGUAGE OF VOCALIZATION

Dogs communicate with the world around them in all kinds of ways. An especially important aspect of canine communication to understand is how they vocalize, which includes barking, growling and whining.

Sometimes excessive vocalization can be annoying, but it's never a good idea to punish your dog for trying to communicate his or her intention. In a best-case scenario, you will damage the ability to communicate effectively with her; in a worst case, punishing any dog for something like growling can be a dangerous move – it might convince her to stop using warning language and progress straight to a bite. The silent aggressive dog is the most dangerous.

Dogs communicate their intentions by how long and how often they bark. For example, if the dog stands squarely while warning you to stay away, she might use a sustained, deep growl. Dogs that growl in shorter bursts are usually more fearful and conflicted about whether to fight or run away if approached. Rapid, higher-pitched sounds indicate excitement or urgency, and a series of intermittent vocalizations means the dog is less interested in a particular situation.

VOCAL COMMUNICATION

RAPID, HIGH-PITCHED = excitement and urgency
SHORT-BURST GROWLS = fearful and conflicted
SUSTAINED, DEEP GROWL = stay away

BARKING

Dogs bark for many reasons, including when they are excited, fearful or anxious or when they desire attention. They bark as a warning or because they're bored. For dogs that bark excessively, the first step is to understand why, because while quick fixes like citronella collars and shock collars might suppress your dog's barking in the moment, they cause more stress and don't work in the long term.[1]

The first step in addressing excessive barking is to make certain that it's actually a problem. In some cases, as guardians we may have our fuses set a bit too short, but in others we may wrongly assume that the persistent canine chatter we find so frustrating is actually very normal and we have to learn to live with it. Yes, it's typical for dogs to bark when the doorbell rings or when they get excited, but excessive barking in any situation is often a symptom of a more serious underlying issue.

BARKING FOR ATTENTION: needy

BARKING FOR ATTENTION

When dogs demand attention by barking, I'm always reminded of a child who constantly tugs on her mother's clothing or interrupts while she is talking. It is just as important to teach your dog some basic manners as it is to teach your child, as long as there is not a more serious reason for their neediness and desire for attention. Dogs that are needy, anxious or stressed are more likely to bark for attention than confident dogs, so it is important to deal with that need first before teaching that barking will not get the attention it desires.

EXCITABLE BARKING

Dogs bark with excitement just as people like to vocalize in exciting situations. This behaviour normally occurs before going for a walk or being fed, which makes it hard to work with, because people usually have a fixed pattern of cues before departure and feeding that are highly ritualized. Dogs pick up on these cues and bark in anticipation.

EXCITABLE BARKING: anticipation of food or walk

ANXIETY BARKING

Some dogs don't like to be alone and become anxious when separated from their humans. Often, these dogs will bark in an effort to re-establish contact or soothe themselves. Lonely/ anxiety barking is usually a series of barks, followed by long pauses as the dog listens to see if her calls have been answered. Lonely dogs sometimes bark for hours until someone responds to them.

ANXIETY BARKING: lonely

BOREDOM BARKING

The garden barker creates an all-too-familiar neighbourhood sound, generally evidence of a dog left alone in the garden or at home all day with nothing to do. Barking can be soothing and gives the dog something to do to pass the time. If your dog is a boredom barker, it's essential you make her day more enriching by hiring a dog walker or taking her to doggy day care. A bored dog should never be blamed for barking when it's the owner's responsibility to make sure all her needs are taken care of.

BOREDOM BARKING: soothing himself

WARNING BARKING: imminent danger

WARNING BARKING

Dogs were the human's first alarm system, and however much we use technology to alarm our homes today, the presence of a barking dog still acts as an effective deterrent. Warning barks are at their most urgent when a visitor comes to the door or onto the property. These barks are usually rapid and lower pitched, communicating that there is imminent danger, unlike the rapid, higher-pitched barks that indicate a dog is excited to greet somebody. Excitement barks usually stop once the visitor is identified and accepted as non-threatening.

HOW CAN I STOP MY DOG FROM BARKING SO MUCH?

The best prescription to modify barking of any sort is to make sure your dog is getting everything she needs in terms of emotional support and security. Exercise and enrichment will help reduce barking in all dogs, especially the bored, lonely or anxious barker. Finding an activity or doing something your dog really enjoys and enriching her life inside the home as well as outside is the key to having a more confident and quieter dog. Try hiding her toys or food around the house and encouraging her to seek them out. Feed her through activity toys at mealtimes instead of in a bowl, so she has to work to find and eat her food. These are all great ways to give her the enrichment she needs. Other ways to manage a lonely dog include enrolling her in a day-care service or having someone play with her during the day – these will minimize her need to bark and seek reattachment. And there is absolutely no justifiable reason to leave your dog out alone in the garden all day – it's not good for your dog or for your neighbours!

GROWLING

It can be frightening when a dog growls or bares her teeth at you, but I would rather that a dog warn me to stay away by growling at me than going straight to a bite. If your dog growls at you, she is likely trying to warn you that something you're doing is making her nervous or uncomfortable, so pay attention. It's normal to want to punish a growling dog, but the fallout is much worse. If a dog is continually punished for growling, she will soon learn to suppress warning language and go straight to more offensive language such as biting. These dogs are much more dangerous.

Some dogs will also growl during play or when they are overly excited. These vocally expressive dogs rehearse growling language without the usual intention behind it, but if the growling becomes too fierce – for example, the body becomes more tense and the pitch of the growl gets lower and continuous, with short intakes of breath that gradually escalate the pitch of the growl – the dogs' intentions have changed, and both dogs should be given a break.

GROWLING: warning of nervousness or discomfort; 'back away'

WHINING

Pups whine from an early age to express their need for a resource or attention. While the sound can be irritating to humans, it is a vital communication signal and shouldn't be ignored. Dogs whine when they are hungry,

WHINING: a need for a resource or attention

thirsty or bored, when they need to go outside, or if they are in pain, stressed or lonely. Whining is a normal vocalization, and the intensity usually fades as a pup grows and becomes more confident.

HOWLING

While domestic dogs bark a lot more than wolves or their wild ancestors, they howl a lot less simply because there is less need. Howling is usually a social signal to gather others together or to establish territorial boundaries – however, though some dogs may howl to establish social contact when alone, most lonely dogs usually bark. Some dogs howl while a person is singing or while a musical instrument is being played. It could be that the tone and pitch of the music encourages this behaviour or that the dog is simply 'singing' along with her social group. If one dog from a multi-dog household howls, others in the social group will usually join her.

HOWLING: social signal

CHAPTER 10

THE LANGUAGE OF PAIN

It is well documented that dogs are sentient beings that experience emotions and physical pain, and there are many similarities between the way humans and dogs experience physical pain. These behaviours include withdrawal from socializing, a higher heart rate and in some cases an increase in vocalizations. Pain is processed in similar parts of the brain in both humans and dogs.

Another intriguing component of pain in animals is that prey animals and predatory animals will often respond to pain differently. As a survival mechanism, prey animals will often show minimal signs that they're experiencing pain. However, predatory animals such as humans and dogs are more likely to show outwards signs of pain. This is why behaviour experts will often recommend a veterinary check at the first sign of aggressive behaviour in dogs. Often pain will manifest as seemingly unprovoked aggression, which can deteriorate over time if the medical issue is left untreated.

The Glasgow Composite Pain Scale is a tool used to assess pain in domestic animals. Veterinarians will take into account several factors to help them determine the level of pain an animal is experiencing. The six categories used to determine pain level include vocalization, attention to a wound, mobility, response to touch, demeanour and posture/activity.[1]

Acute pain comes on quickly as a result of infection, injury or surgery, while chronic pain usually develops slowly and is long lasting. Arthritis is a common source of chronic pain, particularly in elderly dogs. It can go undetected for years as the dog learns to use coping strategies that mask the signs, making finding the source of pain very difficult. In general if you notice a change in your dog's behaviour or she starts moving in a different way (often known as 'pain guarding', which takes pressure off a part of the body that is painful), this could be a sign that she is suffering.

Pain manifests in different ways, but the following are some common signs. If you notice any of these, take your dog to the veterinarian immediately.

- RELUCTANCE TO BE HANDLED OR GROOMED. When dogs show discomfort at being touched or groomed by growling, snapping or biting, they are often admonished for their 'dominant' or 'bad' behaviour, but the truth is that picking up, handling or grooming can be very uncomfortable for some dogs, and the only way the dog can get you to stop is by using warning behaviours. If a dog is experiencing pain in her muscles, or myofascial pain that produces skin sensitivity or hyperalgesia, she might react negatively to being handled. Always give your dog the benefit of the doubt, and to rule out behavioural issues, take her for a full medical check or to a canine masseuse who can diagnose and treat these issues.
- DIFFICULTY IN GETTING UP FROM A RESTING POSITION. Elderly dogs usually take longer to rise from a lying or sitting position – a definite sign that the joints are aching, potentially due to conditions such as arthritis. Dogs that change their sitting position or favour one hip over the other might be doing so because these positions are just more comfortable, or relieve discomfort.
- CHANGE IN BODY POSTURE. Dogs that are in pain will hold their tails differently, or their body will be stiff and less fluid. A dog that has a stomach ache, for example, might arch her back in an attempt to relax the muscles in her tummy.
- CHANGE FROM NORMAL WALKING GAIT. The most visible change in walking gait is lameness, favouring a particular leg, or stiffness, but if you notice that your dog is leaning to one side or hopping on a back leg, this could be a sign of discomfort.
- COAT CHANGES. Changes in your dog's coat can indicate a muscular issue due to decreased circulation caused by a trigger point or strain that impedes blood flow to the hair shaft.
- EXCESSIVE LICKING. Most dogs lick themselves regularly to groom and clean, but if you notice an increase in licking herself this could be a response to pain in the area being licked or referred pain – pain arising from some other, hard-to-reach part of the body, eased by licking an associated area.

THE LANGUAGE OF PAIN

ARCHED BACK: attempt to relax tummy muscles for a stomach ache

GAIT TO ONE SIDE: discomfort while walking

- CHANGES IN BEHAVIOUR. If you notice a sudden change in your dog's behaviour that is abnormal for your dog, such as avoiding being handled, withdrawal, depression, irritability, reduced tolerance for social activities, increased restlessness or nervousness, anxiety, or development of phobias, your dog might be experiencing some physical discomfort that manifests in unusual behaviour.[2]

If your dog is suddenly reluctant to do things she normally enjoys, such as going for a walk or playing a game of tug, it could be a sign that she is trying to manage pain. Shying away from slippery floors, avoiding walking up stairs or jumping into a car, sitting down when on a walk and refusing to move (often interpreted by people as a dog being 'stubborn') are all red flags and should not be ignored.

MANAGING PAIN

Researchers at the University of Wisconsin Veterinary School studied the effects of controlling or managing pain from injuries, illness and surgical procedures in dogs. They concluded that the 'benefits include improved respiratory functions, decreased stress responses surrounding surgery, decreased length of hospitalization, faster recovery to normal mobility, improved rates of healing and even a decreased likelihood of infection after surgery. Almost all studies show people and animals return to normal eating and drinking habits sooner when given relief from pain.'[3]

Other studies conducted across various species have consistently demonstrated that animals that have had surgery but did not have proper pain management afterwards will show behaviours that indicate they are in pain, and those behaviours subside after they have been given proper pain medication. Fascinatingly, a study out of the University of Bristol showed that when birds showing clinical signs of pain such as having a limp were given the choice of eating food that contained painkillers or eating food that had been left untreated, the birds voluntarily chose to eat the food that contained painkillers.[4]

Treating pain in dogs depends on the cause, severity and whether the pain is acute or chronic. Steroids can help reduce inflammation and provide pain relief, although often NSAIDs (non-steroidal anti-inflammatory drugs) are a better alternative for orthopedic pain as they have fewer side effects. You should always consult with your veterinarian before giving your dog any sort of medication, particularly since many human medications (including anti-inflammatory drugs) can be highly toxic to dogs.

There is also a world of holistic veterinary options out there to complement traditional veterinary medicine. Massage, aromatherapy and acupuncture have yielded positive results, but make sure the practitioner you use is willing to work alongside your veterinarian to ensure the best overall care for your dog.

CHAPTER 11

THE LANGUAGE OF AGEING

Like humans, senior dogs will experience a slowing of their cognitive processes as they age that can affect many aspects of their lives. As well as slowing down physically, older dogs can experience behavioural changes that seem unusual or out of character, which could be a sign of cognitive decline. These changes include:

- Less desire to interact and enjoy activities
- Abnormally long sleep periods, particularly throughout the day
- Toileting accidents in the home
- Depression and avoidance behaviour
- Sudden appearance of anxiety issues such as separation anxiety and aggression
- Confusion in a familiar environment
- Failure to respond to previously known verbal and physical cues
- Irritability and less tolerance for human touch
- Failure to recognize familiar people
- Increased dependency and desire for attention from family members

Canine cognitive decline typically begins to set in at around seven to ten years old. Even though most pet parents recognize the physical signs of ageing, signs of mental decline might be harder to spot or could be misinterpreted. If your dog no longer wants to walk upstairs, this could indeed be because of physical constraints such as sore hips, but they could also be because she has forgotten how. Normal everyday rituals become harder to do because she may not remember where the lead is kept before a walk or may have trouble finding the food bowl.

Canine cognitive dysfunction is a disease in senior dogs that manifests similarly to Alzheimer's in humans. In fact, the same development of beta-amyloid plaques in the brain that cause confusion and memory loss in pets are seen in Alzeimer's patients, too. It is believed that there may be a genetic component, but most cases present in senior dogs, with symptoms gradually increasing over time. A 2011 Australian study revealed that about 14 per cent of dogs develop canine cognitive disfunction, but only about 2 per cent are actually diagnosed with the condition. They also found that the risk increases as a dog ages, with more than 40 per cent of dogs over 15 years old showing at least one of the symptoms.[1]

BOOSTING COGNITIVE HEALTH

There are things you can do throughout your dog's life to help her stay cognitively healthy even into old age. Exercise not only benefits a dog physically but gets the dog into a different environment that challenges and stimulates her senses. Among other benefits, exercise increases the production of serotonin and dopamine, neurotransmitters in the brain responsible for regulating emotions, promoting feelings of pleasure and supporting good motor coordination. Exercise promotes a feeling of calm and lowers stress both in people and in dogs. Make sure the level of exercise is appropriate for your dog's age, stamina level and breed type. Just as in humans, a dog's exercise routine should be moderated as they age. Your dog's organs such as the heart and lungs will lose some function over time. It is likely they will not be able to keep up on long walks or runs any more. Instead, find a more leisurely activity that you and your dog can enjoy together such as short walks or training games.

As I mentioned earlier in the book, scent work is becoming increasingly popular around the world. The activity provides extensive physical and mental stimulation for the dog, making it a great way to burn off excess energy and provide cognitive exercise. Because searches can be conducted just about anywhere, training and learning can happen as part of a dog sport team or as a casual exercise at home. Enhancing your dog's scenting abilities provides a great workout for the brain and is a perfect low-impact activity for the elderly dog.

Sports in general are a wonderful way to bond with your dog and give her exercise and mental stimulation. For example, participating in a sport such as agility promotes teamwork and bonding. Dogs of any age can successfully participate in most sports – again, taking into account age, breed and stamina level.

You can use mealtimes to test your dog's hunting skills. Instead of feeding your dog from a food bowl, feed her from a toy instead. Put her food in a toy or treat ball and hide it around your home or garden so that she has to find her dinner. This allows your dog to use her seeking skills, which promotes healthy brain function.

There are many great puzzles on the market designed specifically for dogs. The levels of difficulty vary, and you can hide food inside these, too. Puzzles enhance a dog's natural problem-solving abilities and are great for maintaining cognitive health.

Good nutrition is vital for cognitive health into old age. The use of medium chain triglycerides (MCTs) helps improve brain function in older dogs.[2] MCTs are a kind of fat most commonly found in palm kernel oil and coconut oil. As pets age, glucose, the brain's main energy source, is less readily taken up by the brain cells, but MCTs provide an alternative source of energy for the brain that can help keep your dog mentally sharp as she ages. Simply adding oils to your dog's existing food can help, but she may be more willing to eat a food with MCTs already added. The addition of fish oil, B vitamins, antioxidants and amino acids such as arginine can also slow the brain's decline as your dog ages. When choosing food for your senior dog, keep away from those with by-products, artificial flavourings, artificial colourings, additives and chemicals. You may also need a lower-calorie food to help counter an ageing metabolism.

Old dogs certainly can learn new tricks, and although learning might be a slower process for a senior pet, age should not be an excuse for cutting back on vital physical and mental engagement. With proper physical and mental stimulation, as well as a diet rich in age-fighting ingredients, you can help delay the cognitive effects of ageing and keep your dog mentally sharp well into her senior years.

CHAPTER 12

STRANGE BEHAVIOUR EXPLAINED

If you've ever been baffled by your dog's behaviour, you're not alone. Dogs engage in all sorts of strange behaviours, from spinning to acting as though they can see or hear things that we can't. Researchers are learning more and more about some of these strange behaviours and how they can be explained.

COMPULSIVE DISORDERS

Spinning, light chasing, flank sucking – what causes a dog to engage in these strange compulsive behaviours? Just as some humans suffer from obsessive-compulsive disorders, dogs too can suffer from canine compulsive disorder (CCD). The disorder often begins as a way for the dog to release stress or frustration, and it can quickly become a compulsion. Some common forms of CCD include spinning or tail chasing, excessive licking, air snapping, shadow or light chasing, and flank sucking.

Although CCD can begin in response to stress or anxiety,

COMPULSIVE SPINNING: soothing himself

research has shown there is also a genetic component, so certain breeds are prone to compulsive behaviours. Doberman pinschers commonly engage in flank sucking, a compulsive behaviour in which the dog sucks on objects or on its own skin, while bull terriers are often found to spin compulsively. Interestingly, in a study in the *Journal of the American Veterinary Medical Association*, most of the dogs affected by CCD were purebreds.[1]

Dogs often begin engaging in compulsive behaviours because they live in a sensory-deprived environment where they don't get adequate physical and mental stimulation and their specific breed or behavioural needs aren't met. These behaviours start as displacement behaviours that may help a dog to soothe himself and lower his stress levels for that moment, but over time the behaviours ultimately cause the dog more stress. One 2012 study published in *PLOS ONE* found that the primary triggers for compulsive episodes were boredom or lack of activities (29 per cent) and stressful events (15 per cent).[2]

Because these behaviours are so deeply ingrained both genetically and behaviourally, medication is often needed to stop the cycle of behaviour. Serotonin-uptake blocking drugs have been found to be clinically effective in treating certain canine compulsive disorders.[3]

TOP TIP

If you have a dog that engages in compulsive behaviours, try increasing his mental and physical stimulation (with care; too much active physical exercise can make some dogs worse), and limit the time your dog is contained in a cage or other small area. Talk to your veterinarian about medication options for more severe cases.

ROLLING IN SMELLY STUFF

Have you ever caught your dog rolling around in the grass, and then quickly realized that he has been rolling in something that smells terrible? Thanks to research, there are a few scientific explanations that may offer some insight into why your dog engages in this unpleasant behaviour.

Some researchers suggest that rolling in a rotting carcass or animal poo is a dog's way of marking his territory by depositing his scent on top of the scent of another animal. Another probable explanation is that the behaviour is a remnant of the dog's wild ancestry, a behaviour that lingers from when canids had to hunt to survive. By disguising their scent with the scent of another animal, particularly a prey animal like an antelope, they would be better prepared to sneak up on their prey without giving off a suspiciously 'predatory' odour.[4]

I also believe that dogs roll in smelly stuff because they like the strong scent and the rolling action makes them feel good, even if it disgusts their human parents!

ROLLING IN SMELLY STUFF: scent marking or scent disguising

TOP TIP

Most people who share their lives with dogs have had to deal with their pet rolling in smelly stuff, and management is really the only way to prevent it. If you allow your dog off the lead in an area with new sights and smells, you may want to condition him to an emergency recall cue that will have him reliably running back to you before he finds a prime spot and starts rolling.

DREAMING DOGS

Do dogs (and other animals) dream? It's a question that has long fascinated both scientists and pet parents alike. A 2001 study of rats by researchers at the Massachusetts Institute of Technology (MIT) suggested that the animals not only dream but dream about past events in the same way that humans do. The researchers took recordings of electrical impulses from the rats' hippocampus, the part of the brain that controls memory, while the rats were awake and matched them to nearly identical impulses that occurred while they were asleep.[5] Because the impulses were so clear and consistent, the researchers could pinpoint the exact part of the maze that the rats were dreaming about.

Considering that dogs have a much more complex brain than rats, and their brains more closely mimic those of humans, it is reasonable to assume that dogs also dream.

Dr Stanley Coren, of the University of British Columbia, suggests that you can physically see when a dog is dreaming, as the dog's eyes may move behind his closed eyelids while he is in a dream state. These eye movements are typical during REM sleep, the period of sleep in which humans dream, as the eyes view the dream images in the same way they view real images of the world during waking hours.[6]

DO DOGS HAVE ESP?

Whether or not animals have some sort of extrasensory perception is a topic that has strong proponents on both sides. Many people can testify to anecdotal evidence of animals 'seeing ghosts', predicting natural disasters and smaller-scale phenomena such as predicting when their guardian will return home.

There has only been limited scientific research conducted on the topic, and much of it is considered pseudoscience.

The concept that animals can predict natural disasters such as earthquakes is a particularly fascinating topic. A 2000 study sought to figure out what sensitivities cause animals to predict these events, and suggested that there were four possible explanations: ground tilting, humidity changes, electrical currents and magnetic field variations.[7] All of these possibilities indicate that animals, including dogs, are able to detect minute changes in the environment that would go entirely undetected by humans.

While there is not a clear answer as to the possible psychic abilities of animals (or humans!), science has confirmed that animals have sensory abilities that far outstrip our own.

COPROPHAGIA

There may be no behaviour that humans find more disgusting in dogs than coprophagia – simply put, a dog eating his own faeces or the faeces of another animal. Why is it that some dogs enjoy this seemingly bizarre and potentially harmful behaviour?

There are a few theories, and the answer may vary from dog to dog. For some dogs the cause could be medical; others might do it purely because they like the taste!

Some dogs learn to eat faeces as a puppy, as nursing mothers instinctively eat the faeces of their pups for two reasons. This practice not only helps keep the environment clean, but also may be rooted in an old survival instinct to hide the smell of the puppies from potential predators. If domestic puppies are raised in a crowded, unclean environment like a puppy mill or a poorly sanitized animal shelter, they may have extensive access to their own faeces or the faeces of other animals, and will pick up the habit out of curiosity, boredom or hunger.

Certain medical conditions can also cause coprophagia. Chronic pancreatic deficiency, malabsorption syndrome and starvation are a few of the conditions that exacerbate the need to eat poo. Researchers believe these malabsorption conditions cause high amounts of undigested food to be released in the stool, which not only makes it a nutritional source for the dog, but also helps to satiate the dog's increased appetite.[8]

TOP TIP

As frustrating as coprophagia may be, punishing your dog will not stop him eating poo and will only make him fear you. The key to stopping coprophagia is to be diligent about keeping your dog away from any and all faeces. This means picking up poo immediately after your dog soils, and possibly keeping him on a lead to prevent him engaging in the behaviour while you are out on a walk.

Sometimes the dog's diet is the culprit. Low-quality commercial dog foods tend to be high in carbohydrates and low in protein and key nutrients that can may make the dog feel hungry or unsatisfied, so he looks for an easy 'ready meal'.

CHAPTER 13

HOW TO SPEAK DOG

It is truly incredible that two very different predatory species have managed to successfully coexist for thousands of years. In this book I have focused more on canine language and how dogs have adapted to human domestic life, but humans have also had to make certain adjustments when living with dogs. Success depends on the ability of both species to cooperate, communicate and understand one another, which is not easy when they don't speak the same language.

Speaking dog is all about making it easier for your dog to understand you as well as taking the time to understand your dog. It begins by creating a bond through play, having fun, and making sure you and your dog have good experiences together, using both vocal and physical language to bridge the human/canine language divide.

Dogs, like humans, process language in the left brain hemisphere and emotional content in the right, suggesting that there is some similarity in how dogs and humans process language. While some people might argue that dogs just respond to tone of voice and non-verbal cues rather than words, studies have shown that dogs turn their head to the right when they hear words without emotions, suggesting the left hemisphere is processing speech, and turn their head to the left when they hear emotional words, suggesting the right hemisphere is processing that content.

There are some dogs like Chaser the Border collie, who is famous for knowing more than a thousand words, understanding verbs, adverbs and prepositions.[1]

LEFT HEAD TURN: processing emotional content
(right hemisphere)

RIGHT HEAD TURN: processing speech
(left hemisphere)

She has also learnt that common nouns can identity different objects; for example, a ball is round and a flying disc is flat. She can make inferences in that she can fetch a new toy with a word she's never heard before and pick that toy out from a pile of familiar ones. It is also remarkable that Chaser can understand sentences and pick out a cue within a sentence. This amazing dog is redefining canine intelligence and taking it to a whole new level.

What does this mean for you and your dog? If your dog is having difficulty understanding you, try changing how you teach her. Even though most dogs are good at following human communicative gestures, your dog might not understand what a point means, for example. However, if you say your dog's name, look at her and then look towards where you are pointing, she is more likely to comprehend what you want her to do.

Your personality has a dramatic impact on your dog's behaviour. Because dogs have adapted to read human signals, they are extremely sensitive to our attentional and emotional states. The more extroverted you are, the more attentive your dog will be; conversely, if you have a more introverted personality that inhibits your communicative abilities, your dog might struggle to understand you.

Some studies suggest that people who are less confident have dogs with more behavioural problems.[2] People who are shy, anxious, tense, neurotic or aggressive may also induce nervousness, anxiety and aggression in their dogs.[3] In my experience, nervous, preoccupied or distracted owners tend to have dogs that are less responsive, but conscientious, attentive handlers tend to have dogs that are easier to teach. The more praise and fewer corrections a person gives their dog, the more responsive their dog will be. Happy, confident people tend to have happy, confident dogs!

Most dogs are comfortable with routines. If your life is disorganized and your timing is erratic, your dog might have more behavioural issues as she copes with your unpredictability. The calmer and more organized you are, the more emotionally stable, focused and confident your dog will be. (This benefit could accrue to you as well!)

Even though dogs respond well to vocal cues, using your body language to communicate is very effective. Active hand and body signals are cues that can be paired with actions and behaviours; when your dog is doing something you don't like, passive behaviour such as simply turning your back and ignoring unwanted behaviour can be more effective than shouting and yelling at her.

Be careful about imposing your own values on your dog, because what you perceive may be very different from what she perceives. For example, you might scold your dog for barking and lunging at other dogs, believing her to be dominant or ill-behaved, when in fact she is reacting out of fear.

You might think she pulls on the lead because she wants to be pack leader, when in reality she pulls because she has four legs and you have two and her natural walking pace is much faster than yours. It may be difficult for you to accept that she has just growled at another dog or has pulled you off your feet, but reprimanding her does nothing to make the situation better, because you haven't provided her with an alternative solution.

Be clear with the gestures and vocal cues that you use. Talk to your dog as much as you want, because even though she might not understand what you're saying, she will certainly recognize the tone and pitch of your voice. However, when you're asking her to respond to a vocal cue, use one- or two-word cues to pair with an action, which will make it easier for her to understand what you need her to do.

Some gestures that mean one thing to you might be interpreted quite differently by a dog, especially if you are a stranger to the dog. Hugging, bending over to greet, stroking a dog on top of the head, sustaining eye contact and kissing can all seem threatening if the dog doesn't enjoy close social contact. In the dog world, dogs put their front paws around each other (hug) only if they're going to fight, mount or mate.

Being stroked on top of the head by a great big hand that extends towards them from a large body leaning over them can make many dogs very uncomfortable, particularly during a greeting scenario. Instead, greet a new dog by allowing the dog to come into your space and smell the back of your hand; proceed to stroke the dog only if she invites you to. This will help her relax and begin to accept you.

HUG: threatening if the dog doesn't enjoy close social contact

Unfortunately, we are very good at encouraging and reinforcing our dogs' unwanted behaviour without realizing we're doing it. Feeding from the table encourages dogs to beg; roughhousing with them encourages them to use their mouths during play, which you may find acceptable but suddenly becomes a problem when a child comes to say hello. Be aware of what you might inadvertently be teaching your dog, and make the necessary adjustments so you don't reinforce behaviour you will later spend valuable time trying to change.

STROKING TOP OF HEAD: can be uncomfortable

Human beings are notoriously inconsistent, especially when it comes to creating boundaries. For example, if you let your dog up on the sofa, make sure the rest of the people in your home are fine with that arrangement. If you invite your dog to jump on you, fully expect her to jump up on other people. Dogs can become anxious and confused when one member of the household allows them to do something but is reprimanded by another, so consistency is very important.

Mimicking some of your dog's body language is fine in some scenarios, particularly if you're playing with her. A play bow is a great way to encourage your dog to start playing, but recognize that some of the more outdated advice, especially when it comes to reprimanding your dog, is wrong. For example, don't put your hand over your dog's muzzle to punish her because you've been told a mother does that to her pups when she reprimands them. A mother uses her mouth over the nose or the back of the neck to keep her pups in line, but your hand does not mimic an actual canine mouth, and your dog is smart enough to know the difference. Don't bunch up your fingers and jab your dog in the side while hissing like a snake; the hands you use in anger are the same ones you use to invite social contact, and every dog needs to see an approaching hand as a good thing rather than something that is going to make them feel bad. When hands are associated with punishment, people get bitten, even when they're trying to express affection.

At the end of the day, people can disagree about which training method is more effective and what treatment is morally and ethically correct, but if dogs could speak our language, I know they would set us straight. I can't imagine any dog that would say they like wearing a prong collar or enjoy being shocked with an e-collar, whether they're a family pet or a working dog. I am certain they would tell people to stop devaluing their intelligence, abusing their trust and hurting them in the name of training. They would tell us that they have the capacity to think, to love and to feel emotions that are very similar to ours, and they love the comfort and safety we provide them. They would say that humans are truly a dog's best friend when humans understand dog language and protect them from harm. As long as you are clear, consistent and kind, 'speaking dog' will come easily to you, and your dog will love you for it.

FINAL THOUGHTS

I hope this book has taught you new and helpful things about what your dog's physical and vocal language means and how you can become an even better friend to her. While the book is limited to what I can fit into the allotted pages, it should leave you with better knowledge and understanding of your dog's experience and provide a good foundation for leading a happy life together. Never stop observing your dog's behaviour and appreciating her rich social language. The relationship you have with her is very special and can only be enriched through greater knowledge and understanding.

ENDNOTES

INTRODUCTION

1. Mike LaBossiere, 'Descartes and My Dog', *Talking Philosophy: The Philosophers' Magazine Blog*, 11 June 2009, http://blog.talkingphilosophy.com/?p=1172.

2. Bonne Beerda et al., 'Behavioural, Saliva Cortisol and Heart Rate Responses to Different Types of Stimuli in Dogs', *Applied Animal Behaviour Science* 58, no. 3–4 (July 1998): 365–81.

3. Meghan Herron et al., 'Survey of the Use and Outcome of Confrontational and Non-confrontational Methods in Client-Owned Dogs Showing Undesired Behaviors', *Applied Animal Behaviour Science* 117, no. 1–2 (February 2009): 47–54.

CHAPTER 1: THE LOVING DOG

1. Ádám Miklósi and József Topál, 'What Does It Take to Become "Best Friends"? Evolutionary Changes in Canine Social Competence' *Trends in Cognitive Sciences* 17, no. 6 (June 2013): 287–94.

2. Kerstin Uvnas-Moberg, 'Role of Oxytocin in Human-Animal Interaction', *People and Animals – for Life. 12th International Association of Human-Animal Interaction Organizations (IAHAIO) Conference, Abstract Book* (Stockholm, Sweden: 2010), 7, http://iahaio.org/files/conference2010stockholm.pdf.

3. Anna Hernádia et al., 'Intranasally Administered Oxytocin Affects How Dogs (*Canis familiaris*) React to the Threatening Approach of Their Owner and an Unfamiliar Experimenter', *Behavioural Processes* 119 (October 2015): 1–5, doi:10.1016/j.beproc.2015.07.001.

4.   Yomayra F. Guzmán et al., 'Fear-Enhancing Effects of Septal Oxytocin Receptors', *Nature Neuroscience* 16, no. 9 (September 2013): 1185–7, doi:10.1038/nn.3465.

5.   Department of Ethology, Loránd Eötvös University, 'Attachment Behavior in Dogs', *Journal of Comparative Psychology* 112, no. 3 (October 1998): 219–29.

CHAPTER 2: THE THINKING DOG

1.   Brian Hare and Vanessa Woods, *The Genius of Dogs* (New York: Plume, 2013).

2.   Ibid.

3.   Stanley Coren, *How Dogs Think* (New York: Free Press, 2004).

4.   Claudia Fugazza, *Do As I Do* (Wenatchee, WA: Dogwise Publishing, 2014).

5.   Temple Grandin, *Animals in Translation* (New York: Harcourt Books, 2005).

6.   Kun Guo et al., 'Left Gaze Bias in Humans, Rhesus Monkeys and Domestic Dogs', *Animal Cognition* 12, no. 3 (May 2009): 409–18.

7.   Victoria Stilwell et al., 'Canine Noise Phobia Series 2011'. www.positively.com/products/cnp/.

8.   C. Linster, 'Hebbian Learning and Plasticity' (lecture 12, Cornell University, Ithaca, NY, accessed 28 March 2016). http://www.nbb.cornell.edu/neurobio/linster/BioNB420/hebb.pdf.

CHAPTER 3: THE EMOTIONAL DOG

1.   Dr Attila Andics et al. 'Voice Sensitive Regions in the Dog and Human Brain Are Revealed by Comparative fMRI', 24, no. 5 *Current Biology* (March 2014): 574–8.

2.   Alexandra Horowitz, *Inside of a Dog* (New York: Simon and Schuster, 2009).

CHAPTER 4: THE SENSING DOG

1.   Jay Neitz, Timothy Geist and Gerald H. Jacobs, 'Color Vision in the Dog', *Visual Neuroscience* 3 (1989): 119–25.

2.   Paul E. Miller and Christopher J. Murphy, 'Vision in Dogs', *Leading Edge of Medicine*, JAVMA 207, no. 12 (15 December 1995): 1623–34.

3. Ibid.

4. Ibid.

5. John W. S. Bradshaw, 'The Evolutionary Basis for the Feeding Behavior of Domestic Dogs (*Canis familiaris*) and Domestic Cats (*Felis catus*)', *Journal of Nutrition* 136, no. 7 (July 2006): 19275–315.

6. Ibid.

7. Stephen R. Lindsay, *Handbook of Applied Dog Behavior and Training, Adaptation, and Learning* (New York: Wiley, 2013).

8. George M. Strain, *Deafness in Dogs and Cats* (Cambridge, MA: CABI, 2011).

9. Linn Mari Storengen and Frode Lingaas, 'Noise Sensitivity in 17 Dog Breeds: Prevalence, Breed Risk and Correlation with Fear in Other Situations,' *Applied Animal Behaviour Science* 171 (October 2015): 152–60.

10. Ibid.

11. A. S. Ahl, 'The Role of Vibrissae in Behavior: A Status Review', *Veterinary Research Communications* 10, no. 1 (December 1986): 245–68.

CHAPTER 5: LATERAL LANGUAGE

1. Lara S. Batt et al., 'The Relationships Between Motor Lateralization, Salivary Cortisol Concentrations and Behavior in Dogs', *Journal of Veterinary Behavior* 4, no. 6 (November 2009): 216–22; L. A. Schneider, P. H. Delfabbro and N. R. Burns, 'Temperament and Lateralization in the Domestic Dog (*Canis familiaris*)', *Journal of Veterinary Behavior: Clinical Applications and Research* 8, no. 3 (May–June 2013): 124–34.

2. Batt et al., 'The Relationships' (2009).

3. Shirley S. Wang, 'The Health Risks of Being Left-Handed', *Wall Street Journal*, 6 December 2011, http://www.wsj.com/articles/SB10001424052970204083204577080562692452538.

4. A. Quaranta, M. Siniscalchi and G. Vallortigara, 'Asymmetric Tail-Wagging Responses by Dogs to Different Emotive Stimuli', *Current Biology* 17, no. 6 (March 2007): R199–201.

5. Marcello Siniscalchi, Angelo Quaranta, and Lesley J. Rogers, 'Hemispheric Specialization in Dogs for Processing Different Acoustic Stimuli', *PLoS ONE* (9 October 2008): e3349, doi:10.1371/journal.pone.0003349.

6. Batt et al., 'The Relationships' (2009).

7. M. Siniscalchi et al., 'Sniffing with the Right Nostril: Lateralization of Response to Odour Stimuli by Dogs', *Animal Behaviour* 82, no. 2 (August 2011): 399–404, doi: http://dx.doi.org/10.1016/j.anbehav.2011.05.020.

CHAPTER 7: THE LANGUAGE OF FEAR

1. N. H. Kalin et al., 'The Primate Amyygdala Mediates Acute Fear and Not the Behavioral and Physiological Components of Anxious Temperament', *Journal of Neuroscience* 21, no. 6 (15 March 2001): 2067–74.

2. Temple Grandin, *Animals in Translation: Using the Mysteries of Autism to Decode Animal Behavior* (New York: Scribner, 2005).

CHAPTER 8: THE LANGUAGE OF AGGRESSION

1. James O. Heare, *Aggressive Behavior in Dogs* (Ottawa: DogPsych Publishing, 2007).

CHAPTER 9: THE LANGUAGE OF VOCALIZATION

1. T. I. Raglus, B. D. Groef and L. C. Marston, 'Can Bark Counter Collars and Owner Surveys Help Identify Factors That Relate to Nuisance Barking? A Pilot Study', *Journal of Veterinary Behavior* 10 (May 2015): 204–9.

CHAPTER 10: THE LANGUAGE OF PAIN

1. J. Reid et al., 'Development of the Short-Form Glasgow Composite Measure Pain Scale (CMPS-SF) and Derivation of an Analgesic Intervention Score', *Animal Welfare* 16, no. 1 (May 2007): 97–104(8), https://www.researchgate.net/publication/40704373_Development_of_the_short-form_Glasgow_Composite_Measure_Pain_Scale_CMPS-SF_and_derivation_of_an_analgesic_intervention_score.

2. Louise Swindlehurst, '10 Ways Dogs Show They Have Muscular Pain and Its Relationship with Behaviour' (lecture, Victoria Stilwell Dog Bite and Behaviour Conference, University of Lincoln, UK, June 2015).

3. S. Coren, 'Do Dogs Feel Pain the Same Way That Humans Do?' *Psychology Today*, 20 September 2011, https://www.psychologytoday.com/blog/canine-corner/201109/do-dogs-feel-pain-the-same-way-humans-do.

4. B. Hothersall et al., 'Development of New Techniques to Assess Pain in Domestic Chickens'. Paper presented at the UFAW Animal Welfare Conference, York, UK, 30 June 2010.

CHAPTER 11: THE LANGUAGE OF AGEING

1. H. E. Salvin et al., 'The Canine Cognitive Dysfunction Rating Scale (CCDR)', *Veterinary Journal* 188, no. 3 (2011): 331–6.

2. Melinda Fernyhough Culver, 'Medium Chain Triglycerides in Companion Animals', ABITEC, an ABF Ingredients Company, n.d., http://www.ethorn.com/files/MCT/The%20Future%20Use%20of%20Medium%20Chain%20Triglycerides_Superzoo%202013.pdf.

CHAPTER 12: STRANGE BEHAVIOUR EXPLAINED

1. K. L. Overall and A. E. Dunham, 'Clinical Features and Outcome in Dogs and Cats with Obsessive-Compulsive Disorder: 126 Cases (1989–2000)', *Journal of the American Veterinary Medical Association* 221, no. 10 (15 November 2002): 1445–52, doi:10.2460/javma.2002.221.1445.

2. Katriina Tiira et al., 'Environmental Effects on Compulsive Tail Chasing in Dogs', *PLOS ONE* 7.7 (26 July 2012): e41684, doi:10.1371/journal.pone.0041684.

3. J. L. Rapoport, D. H. Ryland and M. Kriete, 'Drug Treatment of Canine Acral Lick: An Animal Model of Obsessive-Compulsive Disorder', *Archives of General Psychiatry* 49, no. 7 (1992): 517–21, doi:10.1001/archpsyc.1992.01820070011002.

4. Stanley Coren, 'Why Do Dogs Roll in Garbage, Manure, or Other Smelly Stuff?' *Psychology Today*, 29 July 2009, https://www.psychologytoday.com/blog/canine-corner/200907/why-do-dogs-roll-in-garbage-manure-or-other-smelly-stuff.

5. K. Louie and M. A. Wilson, 'Temporally Structured Replay of Awake Hippocampal Ensemble Activity During Rapid Eye Movement Sleep', *Neuron* 29, no. 1 (January 2001): 145–56.

6. Stanley Coren, 'Do Dogs Dream?' *Psychology Today,* 28 October 2010, https://www.psychologytoday.com/blog/canine-corner/201010/do-dogs-dream.

7. Joseph L. Kirschvink, 'Earthquake Prediction by Animals: Evolution and Sensory Perception', *Bulletin of the Seismological Society of America* 90, no. 2 (April 2000): 312–23.

8. Donal McKeown, Andrew Luescher and Mary Machum, 'Coprophagia: Food for Thought', *Canadian Veterinary Journal* 29, no. 10 (October 1988): 849–50.

CHAPTER 13: HOW TO SPEAK DOG

1. Dr John W. Pilley Jr, *Chaser: Unlocking the Genius of the Dog Who Knows a Thousand Words* (New York: Houghton Mifflin Harcourt, 2013).

2. Victoria Ratcliffe and David Reby, 'Orienting Asymmetries in Dogs' Responses to Different Communicatory Components of Human Speech', *Current Biology* 24, no. 24 (December 2014): 2908–12.

3. Nicholas H. Dodman et. al., 'Comparison of Personality Inventories of Owners of Dogs with and without Behavior Problems', *International Journal of Applied Research* 2, no. 1 (2004): 55–61; A. L. Podberscek and J. A. Serpell, 'Aggressive Behaviour in English Cocker Spaniels and the Personality of Their Owners', *Veterinary Record* 141 (1997): 73–6.

PHOTO CREDITS

ACKNOWLEDGEMENTS

While I cannot begin to thank the mass of people that have inspired me over the years, there are many people who have played an integral part in this book. A huge thank you to everyone at Ten Speed Press for their dedication, including my senior editor, Lisa Westmoreland, senior design manager, Chloe Rawlins, and copyeditor, Kristi Hein. Thanks to Patrick Danforth, Kevin Lowery and Nichole Smith for capturing the true nature of our canine companions through their wonderful photography and to Erin Harvey for sharing your incredible illustrations with us. I could not have done this book without you.

The Secret Language of Dogs would not have come into being without the help of my wonderful husband, business partner and friend, Van Zeiler, and my lovely assistant and director of digital content, Alex Andes. On the sidelines to pick me up when I can write no more is my truly amazing daughter, Alex Zeiler – your beauty and kindness inspire me every day.

Thanks to my lovely family and friends, in and outside of the dog world; your love and friendship mean the world to me. And to everyone who works so hard to make animals' lives better in shelters, in homes and in other countries – you know who you are! Thank you!

Thanks also to Heather Paul from State Farm – you are a true gem – your love of animals and your passion is infectious, as well as your wonderful capacity to make us all laugh. Jerry Means and all the other arson dog handlers and investigators I have had the privilege of meeting and working with as well as Austin Weichsel and Leah Brewer – my respect for you all is immeasurable.

To veterinarians Dr Marty Becker, Dr Kwane Stewart and Marc Abraham and all my VSPDT trainers – your dedication to changing animals' lives for the better is inspiring.

And last but by no means least, thanks to my courageous friends and brothers at the Gwinnett County Sheriff's Department including Sheriff Butch Conway; K-9 handlers and trainers Sergeant Paul Corso and Deputy Sheriff Jason Cotton; and all those in field operations, including you, Mike Baker! Thanks also to K-9 handlers Shawn Humphreys, Heath Zeigler, Marvin Tarver, Neil Butler and Johnathan Thomas as well as all those in law enforcement that I have met while filming my show *Guardians of the Night* – thank you for bringing me into the fold and for showing me a world where true human and canine heroes put their lives on the line every day to protect others.

This book is dedicated to my father-in-law, Van Iden Zeiler Jr. Your kindness and wisdom have influenced me more than you could ever know. You were like a second father to me. I miss you and will love you forever.

ABOUT THE AUTHOR

Victoria Stilwell is a dog trainer and behaviour expert best known as the host of the international hit TV series *It's Me or the Dog*, through which she promotes the power, effectiveness and safety of fear-free, positive dog training. A best-selling author of three books – *Train Your Dog Positively, Fat Dog Slim* and *It's Me or the Dog: How to Have the Perfect Pet* – Stilwell is editor-in-chief of Positively.com, president of the Victoria Stilwell Academy for Dog Training & Behavior, and CEO of Victoria Stilwell Positively Dog Training (VSPDT) – the premier network of world-class positive reinforcement dog trainers.

The recipient of multiple awards and a regular contributor to print, radio, digital and TV media as a dog behaviour expert, Stilwell is committed to helping the cause of animal rescue and rehabilitation and is heavily involved with organizations around the world to increase awareness of puppy mills, dog fighting, animal abuse, pet overpopulation, dog bite prevention and other animal-related causes. Stilwell is a national ambassador for the American Humane Association and serves on the advisory boards of Canine Assistants, RedRover, DogTV, Dognition and The Grey Muzzle Organization. Stilwell lives in Atlanta, Georgia in the USA with her husband, daughter and two rescue dogs.

More info about Victoria and positive training: *positively.com*
Find out more about VSPDT: *vspdt.com*
Learn about the Victoria Stilwell Academy: *vsdogtrainingacademy.com*

INDEX

An Hachette UK Company
www.hachette.co.uk

First published in Great Britain in 2017 by Hamlyn, an imprint of
Octopus Publishing Group Ltd
Carmelite House
50 Victoria Embankment
London EC4Y 0DZ
www.octopusbooks.co.uk

First published in paperback in 2019

ISBN 978-0-60063-592-5

A CIP catalogue record for this book is available from the British Library.

Printed and bound in China

10 9 8 7 6 5 4 3 2 1

Originally published in the United States by Ten Speed Press, an imprint of the Crown Publishing Group, a division of Penguin Random House LLC, New York.
www.crownpublishing.com
www.tenspeed.com

Ten Speed Press and the Ten Speed Press colophon are registered trademarks of Penguin Random House LLC.

Illustrations by Erin Harvey
Cover Photography by Kevin Lowery
Design by Chloe Rawlins

Octopus Publishing Group credits:
Editorial Director Trevor Davies
Senior Editor Pauline Bache
Senior Designer Jaz Bahra
Designer Jeremy Tilston
Picture Library Manager Jen Veall
Production Controller Sarah Kulasek-Boyd